Foundation

Geography in Action

Miranda Ashwell

Series Consultant: Andy Owen

Heinemann Educational Publishers
a division of Reed Educational and Professional Publishing Ltd
Halley Court, Jordan Hill, Oxford OX2 8EJ

OXFORD MADRID ATHENS FLORENCE PRAGUE CHICAGO
PORTSMOUTH NH (USA) MEXICO CITY SÃO PAULO
SINGAPORE KUALA LUMPUR TOKYO MELBOURNE AUCKLAND
NAIROBI KAMPALA IBADAN GABORONE JOHANNESBURG

© Miranda Ashwell, 1996

First published 1996

99 98 97 96
10 9 8 7 6 5 4 3 2 1

ISBN 0 435 35065 X

Designed and produced by Gecko Ltd, Bicester, Oxon

Cover photos by Martin Colston (left) and H-J Colston (right)

Printed and bound in Spain by Mateu Cromo Artes Graficas SA

Acknowledgements

The authors and publishers would like to thank the following for permission to use photographs/copyright
material (the numbers refer to the pages on which material appears).

Elaine Bryan and Neville Fisher, extract, 40; Jerry Connolly, for the adapted extract, 18; European Schoolbooks Ltd,
map, 81; Firestone Maps, map, 88; George Philip Ltd: data, 10, 64, maps, 8; The Guardian, map, 64; Hong Kong Year Book 1994,
extract, 68; ILEA/Harper Collins, diagram, 36; The Independent, extract, 62; The International Tea Committee, data, 58; International
Women's Tribune Centre, data, 30, cartoon, 30; Kenyan Tourist Office, data, 49; Michelin Tyres plc: maps, 86, reproduced by permission
of Michelin from their map no 446, 2nd Edition, Authorization No 145/96; New Era (Namibian Publications), extracts, 6, 15, map, 7;
Newcastle-under-Lyme Borough Council, map, 38; Ordnance Survey: reproduced from the Ordnance Survey mapping with the
permission of The Controller of Her Majesty's Stationary Office © Crown Copyright (398020), on pp. 22, 40; Oxford University Press,
map, 24; Philip Allan Publishers Ltd, maps, 26, 66; Rand McNally, map taken from the Arizona Road Map, 63; Sunworld, extract, 72;
Teaching Geography April 1992, Geographical Association/J Naylor, map, 84; The Times, extracts, 47, 65, 67, 93; World Bank, extract, 71;
World Wide Fund for Nature (WWF UK), extracts, 73, 87; Zed Books: a Report by the Women's Feature Service, extract, 75.

Photographs

Action Aid/Jenny Matthews 30, 32, R E Edwards 33, Jerry Flynn 57; AllSport/Simon Bruty 60; Barnaby's Picture Library
38, 63; Biofotos/Ian Took 51; British Geological Survey 17T; Christian Aid/D K Creavance 34, 35T/B; courtesy of
Stoke-on-Trent City Museum and Art Gallery 40; Department of Lands, Queensland, Australia 27T/B; Earth Images,
Bristol, UK/DRA © 1989 data distributed by SPOT image 78; Environmental Picture Library/Nigel Dickinson 14; FLPA/F
Polking 49B, Leo Batten 76; Frank Lane Picture Agency/R Tidman 6, Mark Newman 9T, M Gore 10, 11 E & D Hosking 12T,
Dembinsky/Susan Blanchet 24, Leo Batten 25, W Wisniewski 49T, M J Thomas 61, Celtic Pictures 66, American Red Cross 68,
Panda photo 72, B B Casals 85B, W S Clark 86; Guzelian Photography/Justin Slee 47; Robert Harding Picture Library 80, 81;
Holt Studios/Nigel Catlin 77; Image Bank/Bernard van Berg 85T; J Allen Cash 16R, 71, 73, 82T/B; Neil Pryde Ltd, Hong Kong
45R; Andy Owen 17B, 18, 19, 20T/B, 21, 23T, 23B, 41T/B, 42B, 43L/R, 44, 45L, 74, 89B; Oxfam/Geoff Sayer 52, 53, 54, 56T;
Panos Pictures/Geoff Barnard 13, Borje Tobiasson 29, J Hartley 56B; Planet Earth Pictures/Carol Farreti, 9B, Jeannie MacKinnon
50, John Lythgoe 75; Reuter/Popperfoto 65, 69; Robert Harding Picture Library/Louise Murray 16L, David Beatty 37, Nigel Blythe
42, Sotik Sassoon 59, 78T; Robert Frerck 83, David Hughes 88, Peter Higgins 89T; R M Sanders 61T; courtesy of SEAT UK Ltd
90; courtesy of Newcastle-under-Lyme Borough Council 39; Still Pictures/Edward Parker 12B; courtesy of Trocaire 46.

The publishers have made every effort to trace the copyright holders, but if they have inadvertently overlooked any,
they will be pleased to make the necessary arrangements at the first opportunity.

How to use this book

Location globe
The country you are studying is shown on a map of the world.

Unit aims
The main ideas are found at the start of each unit.

Keywords
Important words are printed in **bold**. These words are explained in the Glossary at the back of the book.

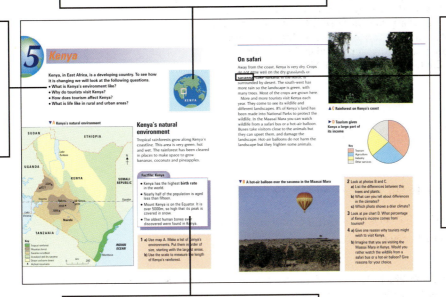

Factfile
Extra facts are given here.

Captions
All the pictures, graphs, maps, and newspaper articles have a caption. The letter next to the ▶ helps you to find the right source when you answer the questions.

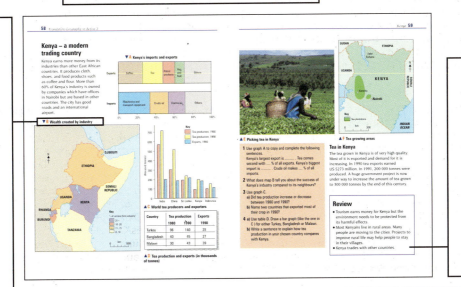

Review
This reminds you about the key ideas. It helps to read the review before you move on.

Index
This lists the topics, places, and ideas covered in the book. It gives the page numbers where they are described.

$\mathcal{C}$ontents

1 Global environment

Tropical rainforests cover only 6% of the land on Earth, yet about half of the world's species of wildlife live there. These rainforests are being destroyed very quickly.
- What are rainforests like?
- Why are they important?
- How are rainforests changing?
- How can they be protected?

GHANA

The disappearing forests of West Africa

Tropical rainforests once grew in a wide belt along the West African coast. Birds, animals, insects and reptiles lived amongst the trees. Today, much of the forest has been burnt or cut down. The wildlife has lost its home.

Where the parrots call no more

In the last 50 years the West African Republic of Ghana has lost 90% of its forest. Much of it has been used for **logging**, when trees are cut down and sold as timber. Trees are also used for firewood and building. The government is trying to keep what is left. 11% of the land is now forest reserve and another 5% is wildlife reserve. Some of the forest is still unprotected.

▼ **A** African grey parrots used to be common in Ghana

▲ **B** Extract adapted from *New Era*, 17 December 1992

▼ **C** Owusu

My name is Owusu. I'm the chief of my village in Takoradi, Ghana. There used to be forest all around. As a boy I could hear parrots calling on the edge of the village. Now they have all gone. Not one can be heard.

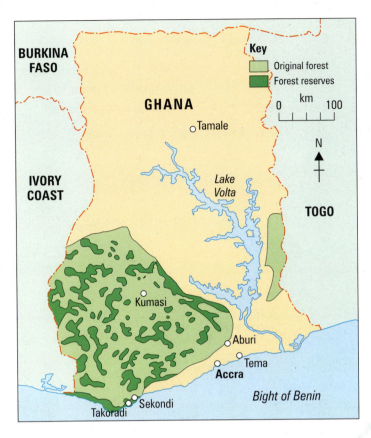

◄ **D** All that is left of Ghana's rainforest

▼ **E** Owusu explains why the forest was destroyed

> The villagers take firewood from the forest. They use fires for cooking and warmth. People also cut wood to build fences and houses. As the village grows, more forest is cleared so that more crops can be grown. The forest was huge. We didn't think that, bit by bit, we were destroying our forest.

Why was so much rainforest destroyed?

Owusu is angry and sad that so much of the rainforest has been destroyed. We shall see how people are trying to protect what is left. Why has this destruction happened?

▼ **F** The growth of Ghana's population

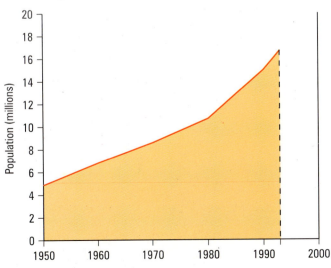

1 Use extract B and E. Copy and complete the following sentences.
Ghana is a country in .... About ...... % of its rainforest has been lost. It was used for ...... , ... and buildings.

2 Look at map D. Name a town that has lost the rainforest that once grew around it.

3 Give three reasons why the forest has been destroyed.

4 a) What was Ghana's population in 1950?
   b) What was Ghana's population in 1990?
   c) Work out Ghana's population growth between 1950 and 1990.
   d) How did Ghana's population growth affect the forests?

5 What has happened to the parrots that Owusu used to hear?

Where do tropical rainforests grow?

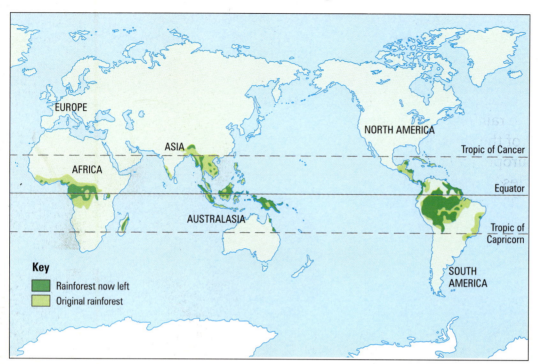

◀ **A** Tropical rainforests: where they used to be, and how much is left

Key
- ■ Rainforest now left
- ■ Original rainforest

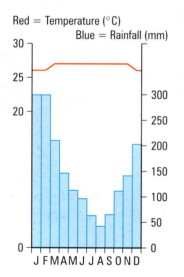

Red = Temperature (°C)
Blue = Rainfall (mm)

◀ **B** The tropical climate of Jakarta, Indonesia.

Map A shows that rainforests grow near the **Equator**. The temperature there stays almost the same all year round. Plants grow well in this hot, steamy **climate**. Animals can find food, such as fruit, flowers and leaves all through the year. Two main types of rainforest grow around the Equator.

- Lowland forest. The Amazonian rainforest in South America, for example, is the largest rainforest in the world.
- Mountain rainforests. In these forests the trees are shorter, with smaller leaves. Zaire has mountain rainforests.

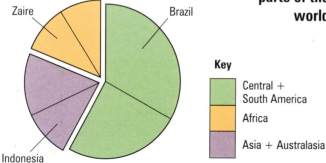

▼ **C** Most rainforest that is left is shared between three parts of the world

Key
- ■ Central + South America
- ■ Africa
- ■ Asia + Australasia

1 Use map A and pie chart C to complete the following sentences:
The continent that has the most rainforest is .... Zaire has the most rainforests in .... Rainforests are found near the Equator between the Tropic of .... and the .... of Capricorn.

2 Use graph B to describe the climate of Jakarta. Mention:
a) the amounts of rain at different times of the year
b) the temperature pattern throughout the year.

The rainforest ecosystem

Plants and animals need each other for food and shelter. They also depend on the **weather** for warmth and water. We call this relationship an **ecosystem**.

Tropical rainforests have a huge variety of wildlife species. This means that the rainforest ecosystem is complicated. About half of the world's wildlife lives in the rainforest. In Europe, one hectare of wood has only twelve species of tree. One hectare of a tropical rainforest has 230 species of tree. Thousands of birds and animals, and millions of insects live amongst these trees.

► E
Orang-utans are well adapted to life in the rainforest canopy

▼ **D The rainforest ecosystem**

Canopy

Their goodness is taken into the tree through its roots.

They are quickly broken down by beetles, fungi, and bacteria.

Leaves and branches fall from the trees all through the year

1 The trees form a **canopy**. This breaks up the force of the rain. It stops the soil below from being washed away by heavy rain.

2 Birds and monkeys live in the canopy. They eat fruit and flowers in the trees.

3 The canopy stops most of the sunlight reaching the ground. It also traps the warm, damp air below.

4 Animals such as jaguars hunt on the dark forest floor.

▲ F. **Many rainforest flowers, such as this orchid, have bright colours**

3 Give two reasons why plants grow well in rainforest climates.

4 Imagine that you are an orang-utan and describe your life in the rainforest.

5 Draw or make a collage of a rainforest, adding labels to explain the rainforest ecosystem.

Developing the rainforest

Graph A shows that tropical rainforests are being destroyed all over the world. We will see how rainforests are used as a resource and will look at the ways they are used in different countries.

▼ **C**
Using the rainforest

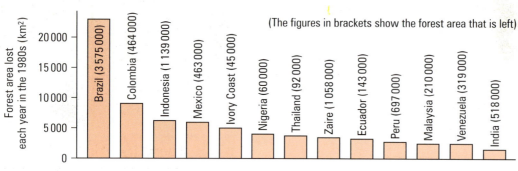

(The figures in brackets show the forest area that is left)

Forest area lost each year in the 1980s (km²)

Brazil (3 575 000)
Colombia (464 000)
Indonesia (1 139 000)
Mexico (463 000)
Ivory Coast (45 000)
Nigeria (60 000)
Thailand (92 000)
Zaire (1 058 000)
Ecuador (143 000)
Peru (697 000)
Malaysia (210 000)
Venezuela (319 000)
India (518 000)

▲ **A** **Rainforest lost each year**

2 Logging: This means cutting down trees for sale as timber. Big companies pay for the right to cut logs from the forest. Many trees are cut down just to make room for the lorries and machines.

▼ **B** **Forest logging in Liberia, Africa**

Factfile: Logging

- 40% of rainforest destruction is caused by the logging of hardwoods.
- Most tropical hardwood is sold to Japan and the European Union.

5 Hydro-electric power (HEP): Some areas of rainforest are flooded by huge reservoirs. They are built to provide cheap hydro-electricity.

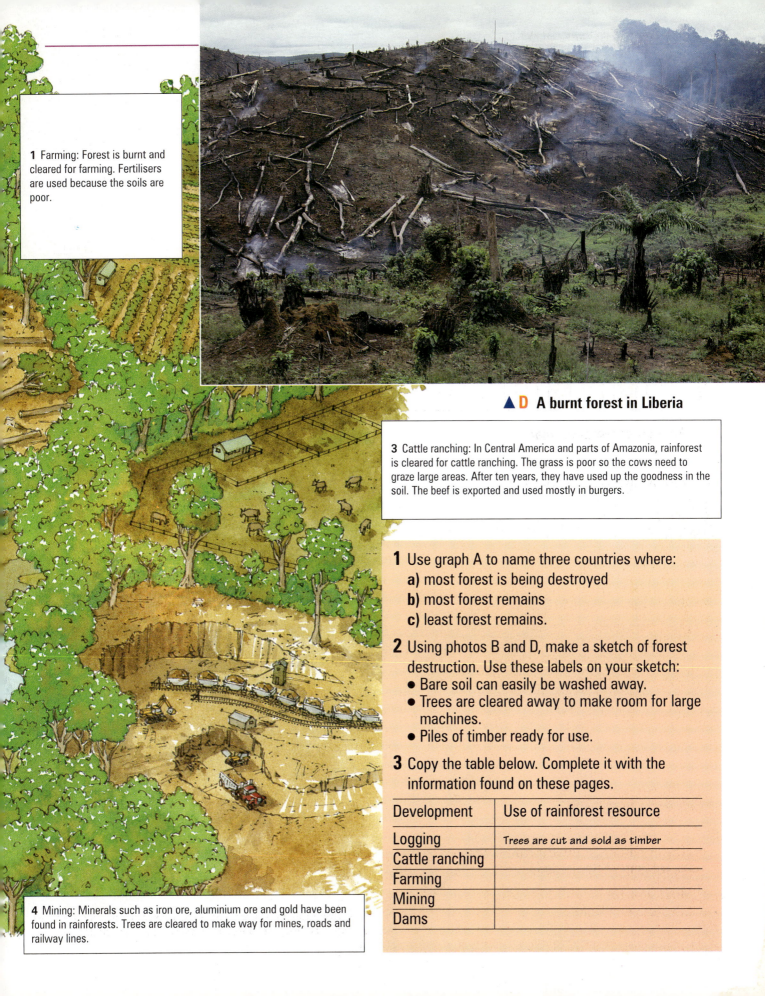

1 Farming: Forest is burnt and cleared for farming. Fertilisers are used because the soils are poor.

▲ **D** A burnt forest in Liberia

3 Cattle ranching: In Central America and parts of Amazonia, rainforest is cleared for cattle ranching. The grass is poor so the cows need to graze large areas. After ten years, they have used up the goodness in the soil. The beef is exported and used mostly in burgers.

4 Mining: Minerals such as iron ore, aluminium ore and gold have been found in rainforests. Trees are cleared to make way for mines, roads and railway lines.

1 Use graph A to name three countries where:
   a) most forest is being destroyed
   b) most forest remains
   c) least forest remains.

2 Using photos B and D, make a sketch of forest destruction. Use these labels on your sketch:
   • Bare soil can easily be washed away.
   • Trees are cleared away to make room for large machines.
   • Piles of timber ready for use.

3 Copy the table below. Complete it with the information found on these pages.

Development	Use of rainforest resource
Logging	Trees are cut and sold as timber
Cattle ranching	
Farming	
Mining	
Dams	

Is there a better way to use the rainforest?

The rainforest is a rich **environment** that is easily damaged. Can we use the rainforest resource without harming it forever?

Harvesting in the rainforest

Hundreds of forest plants produce fruit, flowers, leaves, nuts or wood that can be used. Look at photo A. Women are preparing Brazil nuts in a factory near the Amazon rainforest. The huge Brazil nut trees take 500 years to grow. Luckily, gathering these nuts does not harm the forest. People have tried to grow Brazil nut trees as a crop but the trees would not produce nuts. They only grow nuts in the forest.

▶ **B** Tribal people know how to use the forest without damaging it

Factfile: Rainforest products

- New medicines, made from rainforest plants, are being found. One of these can treat a type of cancer called leukaemia.

- New types of crops are being grown from wild types found in the forest such as coffee in Madagascar, and maize in Mexico. This maize is not easily affected by drought or disease.

- A survey in Peru shows that more money can be made from natural rainforest products than from timber.

▼ **A** Brazil nut workers in Belém, Brazil

▼ **C** Mixing forestry and farming to help people

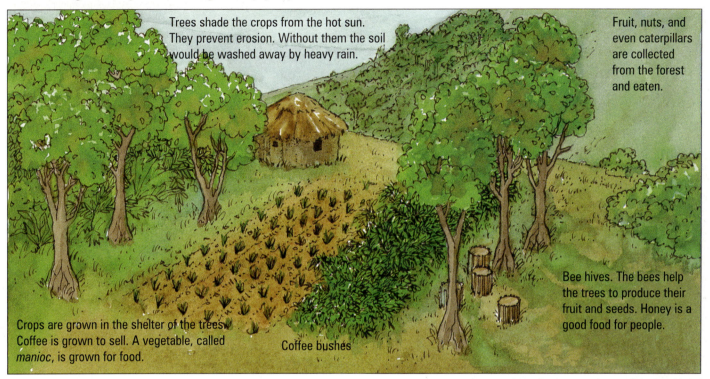

Trees shade the crops from the hot sun. They prevent erosion. Without them the soil would be washed away by heavy rain.

Fruit, nuts, and even caterpillars are collected from the forest and eaten.

Bee hives. The bees help the trees to produce their fruit and seeds. Honey is a good food for people.

Crops are grown in the shelter of the trees. Coffee is grown to sell. A vegetable, called *manioc*, is grown for food.

Coffee bushes

Farming in the forest

In parts of Africa people are farming land without destroying the forest. A few strips of land are cleared on the edge of the forest. Crops are planted in these strips so people can still also collect fruits, nuts, and firewood from the forest. This method of farming is called **agroforestry.** Look at picture C.

▶ **D** Agroforestry – growing spice between the trees in Kerala, India

1 Choose either photo A or B. Imagine that you could visit the people in the photo.
   a) Write a list of the questions you might ask them about their life and work.
   b) Write a list of the activities they might show you.

2 Use picture C to list three advantages of agroforestry.

3 Write a letter to the Minister for Agriculture in a country where the rainforest is being cleared for cattle ranching. Tell him or her:
   a) about the effects of cattle ranching
   b) why agroforestry would be better.

4 Why might the Minister of Agriculture want cattle ranching rather than agroforestry?

How can the rainforest be saved?

Countries with rainforests need to use them as a resource. So how can the rainforests that are left be saved?

▼ **A** Tribal people in Sarawak block a road to protect their forest from loggers

Strip logging

Strip logging lets trees be used for timber but the rainforest can still regrow. Trees are cut in a strip which is 20m wide. Once the timber has been taken away, the clearing is left so that trees and plants can grow there again. Picture B shows how strip logging works.

Advantages:
- Local people can use this method to earn money, rather than large companies.
- Local people can keep their homes and way of life.
- A portable sawmill is carried into the forest by oxen. No roads are built for lorries and big machines. Less damage is done as only a few chosen trees are cut down.

▼ **B** How strip logging works

1 Valuable trees are chosen.

2 They are cut down, cut into planks and taken away by oxen.

3 Seeds blow in and the forest can regrow.

▼ **C** Ideas about using rainforest timber

I buy hardwood from a local firm in Peru. They use strip logging. We must help by buying from them or the big companies will destroy the forest.

I'm a builder. I never buy any tropical hardwood because I'm worried about the rainforests. I use pines from Canada or oak from Europe instead.

Where the parrots call no more

Protecting Ghana's forests is difficult. Only a few rangers look after a huge area of land. 'Officials don't care about a forest that they never visit. They don't earn enough money to live on so it is easy to bribe them,' says one ranger. It is hard to stop this happening.

▲ **D** Extract adapted from *New Era*, 17 December 1992

1 Give one advantage of strip logging:
   a) for the local people
   b) for the environment.

2 Read the opinions of the two men in picture C. Who do you agree with and why?

3 Give two reasons why it is difficult for governments to control logging completely.

4 Use the information in this unit. Discuss what could be done to save the rainforest by:
   a) local people living in rainforest areas
   b) ordinary people, like yourself, living in the rest of the world.

What is being done to save Ghana's rainforest?

- Forest reserves have been set up with rangers to look after them.
- Loggers must now have permission to fell trees.
- Villagers are replacing crops with trees. This is called woodlot farming. The new forest will give firewood, shade, and will help to stop soil erosion.

Review

- Rainforests are a very important ecosystem with a vast amount of wildlife.
- Rainforests are being destroyed because people are using their resources, such as timber and minerals too quickly.
- People are trying to find ways to save the rainforests which are left.

2 Coastal environment

The coast stands between our homes and the sea. It is also a home for wildlife.
If the coast is damaged, people and wildlife are at risk.
- How is the coastline shaped?
- What problems arise as the coast changes?
- How can we look after our coast?

▲ **A** The wild coastline of Scotland

▲ **B** The coast is used as a resource by tourists

An island nation

Britain is an island so no one lives very far from the sea. The British coast has many different types of landscape and habitats as photos A, B and C show. We call the environment where a plant or animal lives its **habitat**.

Losing our coast

Our coast is being eroded or worn away. This **erosion** happens in several ways.
- Waves hit against the rocks and weaken them.
- Air is trapped between the waves and the rocks. This widens cracks in the rocks.
- Waves throw stones and sand onto the shore, slowly breaking it up.
- Over time, a notch (or V-shape) is cut in the shore. The weight of soil and rocks above can make the cliff fall in a **landslide**.

1 List the ways that people use the coast for:
a) leisure
b) work.

2 Use photo C and the scale to measure:
 a) the width of the landslide at its widest point
 b) how close other buildings are to the cliff edge.

▶ **C** In June 1993 Holbeck Hall Hotel fell in a landslide

▼ **D** Thoughts about the collapse of the hotel

We could hear the house moving just hours before it fell.

How awful to lose your home and your business.

I live near the fallen hotel. I'm afraid that no one will ever buy my house.

▶ **E** A small landslide on Charmouth beach

3 Imagine that you are a newspaper reporter. Write an interview with the owner of Holbeck Hall Hotel just after the landslide happened.

4 Write a poem or draw a picture that shows the attractive side of the coast, such as for a holiday or a walk. Do another one showing the dangerous side of the coast, such as a storm or a landslide. Give each poem or drawing a title.

5 Draw photo E. Add these labels:
 ● small landslide
 ● layers of rock in cliff
 ● beach.

Looking after the coast

Landslides and erosion have been happening on the east coast of England for hundreds of years. In Robin Hood's Bay, near Scarborough, 200 houses have fallen from the cliff since 1770. A sea wall has now been built to stop the erosion. But erosion is still a problem for some people as B and C show.

▼ **A** The sea wall in Robin Hood's Bay

Village waits for the cruel sea

Sue Earle is waiting for her home and farm to fall into the sea. Her house is only 16m from the collapsing cliff edge. In a year it will have fallen into the North Sea. Already water pipes have fallen away. Sue will lose her dairy and electricity supply in the next landslide. 'High tides and high winds in winter have the worst effect', says Sue.

The Humberside coast where Sue lives has the fastest coastal erosion in Europe. No money will be paid to Sue when her farm falls into the sea. She will be homeless.

▲ **B** Extract adapted from *The Sunday Telegraph*, 7 August 1994

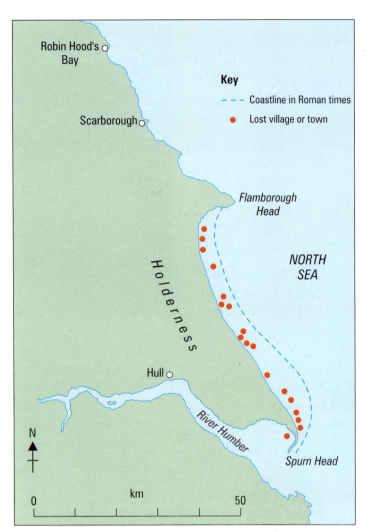

Key
- - - Coastline in Roman times
● Lost village or town

▲ **C** Erosion on the east coast of England

1 Look at map C.
   a) How many settlements have been lost?
   b) Measure the length of coastline that has suffered from coastal erosion.
   c) What damage has happened to houses along the Holderness coast?

2 Draw a sketch of map C. Add labels to show that:
   • The Holderness coast is made of soft loose clay which is easily eroded.
   • Flamborough Head is made of chalk which does not erode so quickly.
   • Eroded clay is carried down the coast and dropped at Spurn Head.

Defending the coast

To protect land and property, erosion can be slowed down or prevented. Britain spent £300 million in 1994 defending the coast. Picture D shows some of the ways that coastal erosion can be prevented.

▼ **D** Some of the ways to prevent erosion

1 Pile up rocks or concrete blocks.	**2** Add new sand to build up a beach.	**3** Build groynes down the beach.	**4** Build a sea wall.
Blocks break up the strong waves but they look ugly. They make it hard to get onto the beach.	The beach soaks up the wave energy. This works well but it costs money.	Groynes are walls built down the beach which help to keep sand on the beach. Rock groynes are expensive. Thousands of timber groynes in the UK need repair.	A sea wall works well for a few years, but is very expensive to build and needs to be repaired.

▼ **E** Mending a groyne in Sidmouth, Devon

3 Copy the table below and fill it in using information from picture D.

Type of defence	How it works	Good points	Bad points
Piles of rock			
New sand			
Groynes			
Sea walls			

4 Which types of defence would cause fewest problems for people using the beach?

5 Look at photo E. Why might this work be difficult on the beach?

The beach environment

Waves carry sand or shingle along with them. When a wave runs out of energy, this sand and and shingle is dropped. We call this **deposition.** This makes a beach. A beach defends the land against flooding and erosion.

Plants that like a sandy, salty habitat **colonize** or take over the top of the beach. Many coasts are good places for wildlife.

▲ **B Salt marsh**

▼ **A The Dyfi Estuary, Wales**

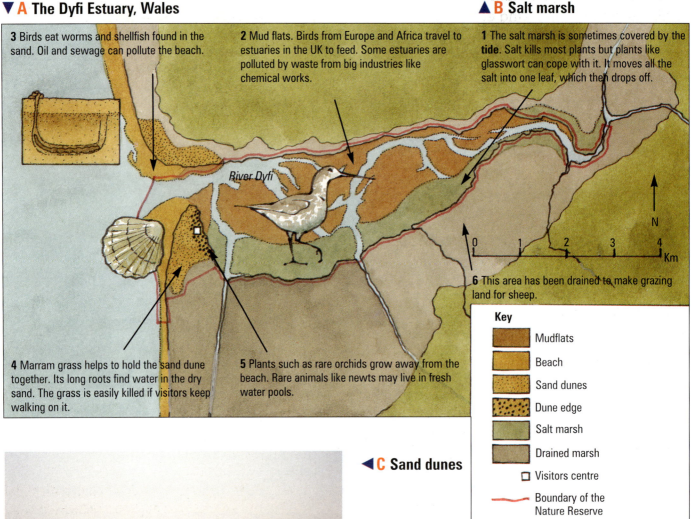

3 Birds eat worms and shellfish found in the sand. Oil and sewage can pollute the beach.

2 Mud flats. Birds from Europe and Africa travel to estuaries in the UK to feed. Some estuaries are polluted by waste from big industries like chemical works.

1 The salt marsh is sometimes covered by the **tide.** Salt kills most plants but plants like glasswort can cope with it. It moves all the salt into one leaf, which then drops off.

River Dyfi

N

0   1   2   3   4 Km

6 This area has been drained to make grazing land for sheep.

4 Marram grass helps to hold the sand dune together. Its long roots find water in the dry sand. The grass is easily killed if visitors keep walking on it.

5 Plants such as rare orchids grow away from the beach. Rare animals like newts may live in fresh water pools.

Key

▨	Mudflats
▨	Beach
▨	Sand dunes
▨	Dune edge
▨	Salt marsh
▨	Drained marsh
☐	Visitors centre
⎯	Boundary of the Nature Reserve

◄ **C Sand dunes**

1 Copy the sentences below. Fill in the gaps using the words below.
A wave carries sand or .... When it runs out of ...... the wave ...... the sand. This is how a ...... is made. We call this ....

deposition energy drops beach shingle

Looking after coastal environments

Each winter thousands of birds fly to the Dyfi river **estuary** in Wales. Picture A shows the Dyfi Estuary. Each summer thousands of people visit the beach and sand dunes at the estuary mouth. When people walk through the sand dunes to reach the beach they can trample on the plants. This kills the plants, and lets the wind erode the dunes, as picture D shows.

The sand dunes and salt marsh are a National Reserve. Wardens protect it by:

- fencing off areas that are easily damaged
- building wooden paths
- showing people how to look after the dunes.

▼ **D** How the dunes are eroded

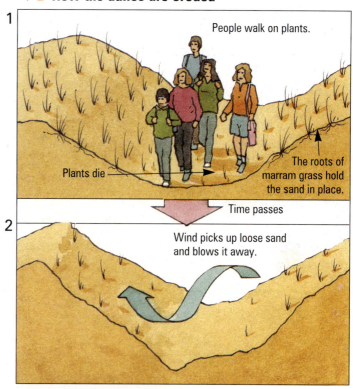

1 People walk on plants.

The roots of marram grass hold the sand in place.

Plants die

Time passes

2 Wind picks up loose sand and blows it away.

◄ **E** A wooden path should stop people trampling the dunes

2 a) Look at map A. List three environments which are protected within the nature reserve.

b) Explain how each of the environments on your list can be damaged by people.

3 Discuss the ways in which wardens try to reduce the damage done by visitors.

4 Sketch photo E. Add labels to show where:
a) erosion might happen
b) erosion is being prevented
c) people try not to damage the dunes.

5 There are no litter bins in the reserve, but litter is not a problem. Discuss why wardens might not put out bins.

The Jersey coast

Jersey is one of the Channel Islands which French and British people visit on holiday. The map and photos show the south-west part of the island.

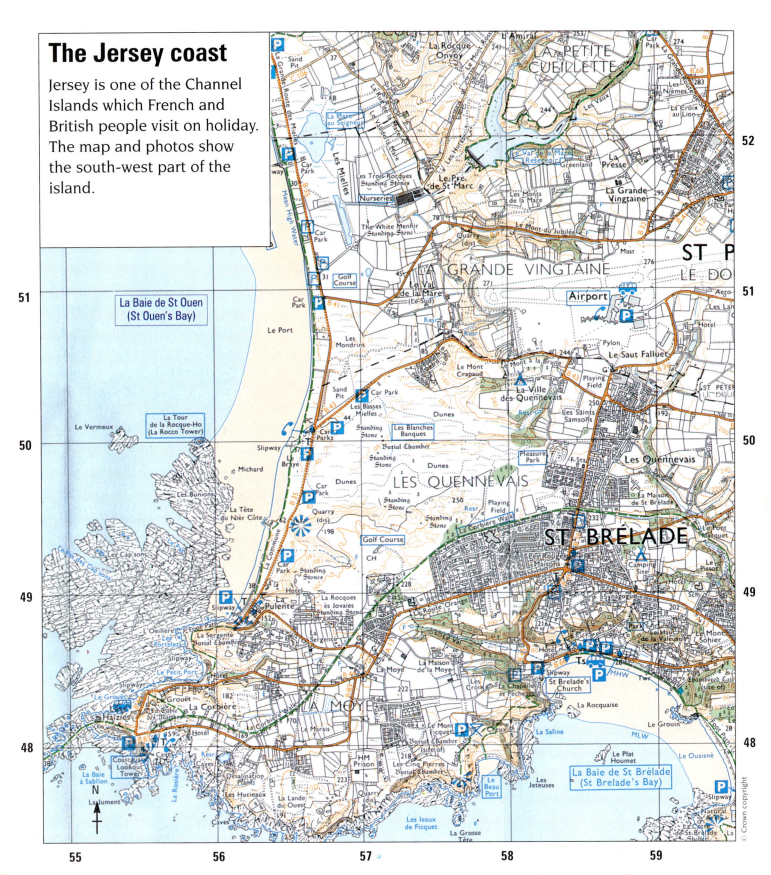

▲ **A** The south-west coast of Jersey in the Channel Islands. Ordnance Survey map at 1:25 000

◀ **B** The beach of St Oeun's Bay. This photo was taken from grid reference 566494 on map A

▲ **C** Rocky coast, La Grosse Tete (577478 on map A)

Jersey is made of granite, a hard rock that does not easily erode. There are crystals in the rock. These are broken down in a chemical reaction with rainwater. Over hundreds of years the rock is weakened. This is called **weathering.**

Weathered granite can be eroded by sea waves. The broken pieces are then worn smooth in the sea and become sand. This sand is then deposited to make sandy beaches.

1 Match the following words with their meaning.
deposition   when soil or rocks are worn away by wind or moving water
erosion   breaking up of rocks by the weather, such as rain
weathering   when silt or sand is dropped by waves or rivers.

2 Look at photo B.
  a) Using the word 'weathering', explain how the sand has been made.
  b) Using the word 'deposition', explain how the beach has been made.

3 Use map A and photo B. Copy the sentence below choosing the right word.
The camera that took photo B was pointing *south/north/east/west*.

4 Using the map and photos:
  a) describe three things tourists would like about this coast
  b) name three places that a tourist might visit and give their grid references.

5 Design an information board that could be put up in the dunes at grid reference 5750. It should show visitors how to take care of the environment. Use pictures, maps or diagrams to help get your message across.

Tropical coastlines

We have seen how the coast of the British Isles changes and how this environment can be harmed by people. We will see how tourism can harm the wildlife and environments of tropical coasts.

Coral reefs

A **coral reef** is an ecosystem with many plant, animal and fish species. Coral is made of masses of tiny animals, each covered in hard lime. Together they build up to form a reef. These reefs are found only in clear, shallow warm waters.

Mangroves

Mangrove trees grow along shallow coasts in some tropical countries. Their roots trap mud and sand and stop it from being washed out to sea. This protects the coast from erosion.

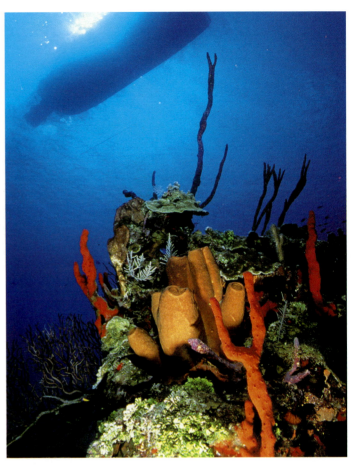

▲ **A** Coral on the Caribbean reef

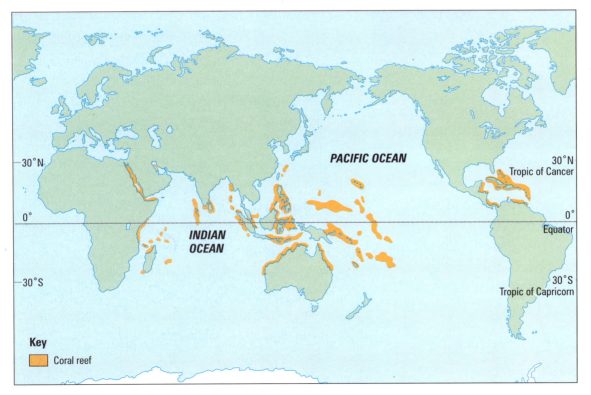

◄ **B** The location, or place, where coral reefs are found around the world.

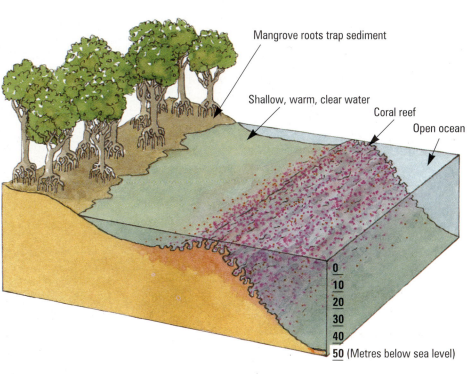

Mangrove roots trap sediment

Shallow, warm, clear water

Coral reef

Open ocean

0
10
20
30
40
50 (Metres below sea level)

▲ **C** Mangroves in Florida in the USA   ▲ **D** A tropical coastline

Why coral reefs are important

Coral reefs protect the coast from waves and erosion. Thousands of fish and other sea animals live amongst the coral. Reefs also provide a home for young fish which are later caught and eaten by local people. Some corals make chemicals which people find useful.

Coral reefs and mangroves are in danger from tourist resorts.

- Trees that hold the soil together are cut down so that hotels and roads can be built.
- When these trees are gone, rain washes the soil into the rivers. The rivers take **sediment** such as mud and silt to the sea. The sediment covers and kills the coral reef.
- **Pollution**, for example raw sewage from hotels, can also kill the reef.

1 Use map B and diagram D. Copy the following sentences and fill in the gaps:

Corals only grow in shallow water that is .... and .... They are found in the P....... O....... and off the coast of South East A....... . They are made of tiny .... covered in hard ....

2 a) List three reasons why coral reefs are important.
b) List three ways in which tourism can harm coral reefs.

3 Copy diagram D. Add labels to show what happens when tourist resorts are built on the coast.

Managing the Great Barrier Reef

The Great Barrier Reef in Australia is the largest coral reef in the world. It has been made a World Heritage Site and a Marine Park. The job of the Marine Park Authority is to:

- protect the reef from damage by people
- let scientists learn more about the reef
- allow tourism on or near the reef.

Pressures on the reef

More and more tourists are visiting the reef. Photos D and E show some of the developments that have taken place. Cairns airport, for example, is bigger now. There are also new hotels, resorts and roads. Tourists take trips into the rainforest behind the hotels. They can also take boat trips to the reef to swim, snorkel and dive.

▼ **A** Location of the Great Barrier Reef

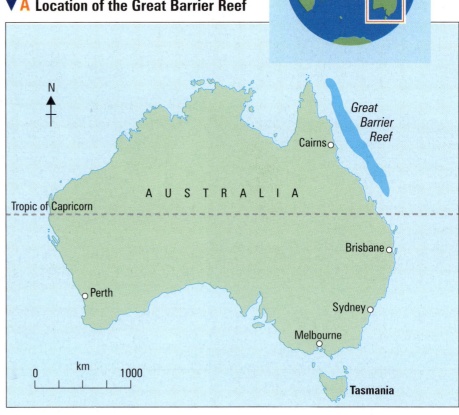

▼ **B** Passengers at Cairns Airport

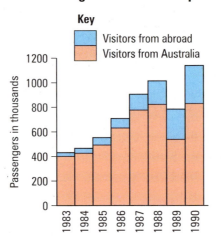

▼ **C** Where visitors came from in 1990

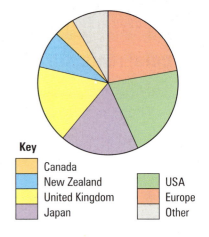

Key
- Canada
- New Zealand
- United Kingdom
- Japan
- USA
- Europe
- Other

1 Look at map A. How long is the Great Barrier Reef?

2 Give reasons why the reef was made into a Marine Park.

3 Use bar graph B. How many more tourists visited in 1990 than in 1983?

Factfile: The Great Barrier Reef

- It is the largest protected marine area.
- It has 400 different corals.
- It has 1500 different species of fish.
- Turtles, whales and dolphins visit the reef.

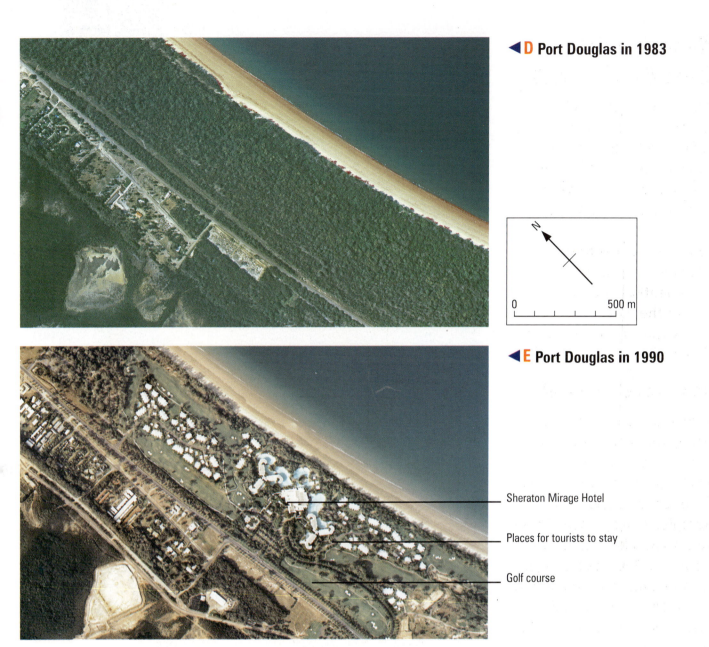

◀ **D** Port Douglas in 1983

◀ **E** Port Douglas in 1990

Sheraton Mirage Hotel

Places for tourists to stay

Golf course

4 Use chart C. Where did most tourists come from?

5 Look at photos D and E.
   a) Describe what has happened to the forest.
   b) List the other changes that you can see.
   c) How might these changes affect the natural environment?

Review

- Coastal landscapes are easily eroded. We need to defend our land against coastal erosion.
- There are many different coastal environments, such as sandy beaches, rocky cliffs, mangroves and coral reefs.
- People can damage coasts through development or pollution. The growth of tourism can be a danger to our coasts.

3 Rural development

In developing countries people are moving from the rural areas to the cities. They are looking for a better way of life.
- Why does this happen?
- How can life in rural areas be improved?

SOUTH-EAST ASIA

▼ A The growth of Bombay's population

▼ B People moving to Asia's cities

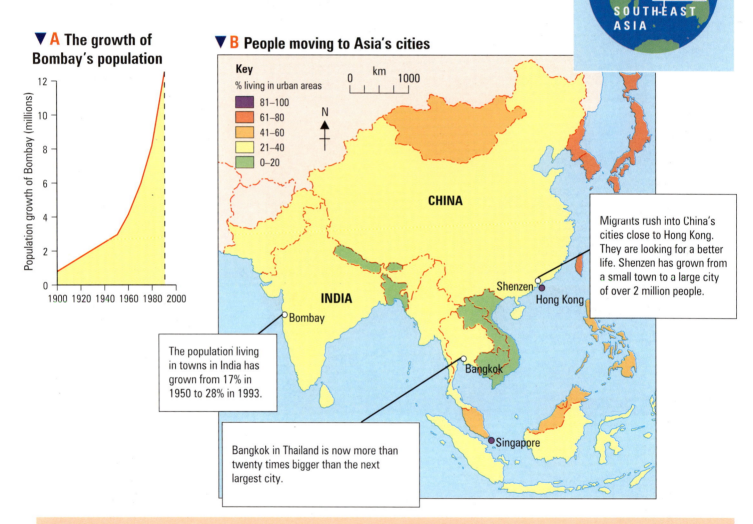

Key
% living in urban areas
- 81–100
- 61–80
- 41–60
- 21–40
- 0–20

km
0   1000

N

CHINA

INDIA

Bombay

Shenzen

Hong Kong

Bangkok

Singapore

Migrants rush into China's cities close to Hong Kong. They are looking for a better life. Shenzen has grown from a small town to a large city of over 2 million people.

The population living in towns in India has grown from 17% in 1950 to 28% in 1993.

Bangkok in Thailand is now more than twenty times bigger than the next largest city.

1 Use map B and an atlas to find a country where:
   a) over 60% of the people live in cities
   b) between 21% and 40% of the people live in cities.
   c) under 20% of the people live in **rural areas**.

2 Use map B and an atlas to complete the table. What do you notice?

Country	Wealth (**GNP**)	Percentage of people living in cities
Nepal	$ 180	
Bangladesh	$ 220	
Taiwan	$ 8 000	
Japan	$26 920	

Why do people move?

Bombay in India is one of Asia's fastest growing cities. People move there from other areas. This is called **migration**. Why do people migrate, or move, to Bombay?

3 a) Use these figures to draw a line graph of Calcutta's population growth. Use the axes from graph A.

Population of Calcutta (millions)

1901	1951	1961	1971	1981	1991
1.5	4.6	5.7	7.0	9.2	10.9

b) How are the population growths for Calcutta and Bombay similar ?

c) What differences can you see between the two cities? Look at how each graph starts and finishes.

4 Read what people have to say in D as well as the Factfile. Copy, or write in your own words, the information which shows that:

a) not all migrants live in the city for the rest of their lives

b) migrants plan their move to the city.

5 List the reasons why migrants move to the city.

Factfile: Indian migrants

A study of migrants in Bombay showed that:

● only 15% were unemployed and even they wanted to stay in the city

● 78% stayed with friends or relatives when they first arrived

● some are landless farm workers who work in the city but go back to their village to harvest crops

● most make the city their home and send money back to their families in the country.

▲ **C** Bombay

After reading about Bombay in the paper I decided to move here. I can make three times as much money here as I could in my village. I send most of it home.

I'll do any sort of work. I've carried bricks on a building site. I don't get much money, but I couldn't get any work in the country.

My brother got me a job in a street market. Each year I visit my family in the country for about a month.

▲ **D** Migrants to Bombay explain why they moved

What is rural life like?

In Africa and Asia cities are growing fast but most people still live in rural areas. Rural life is hard, with few things to make life comfortable. Many people own little or no land. Women and children do much of the work.

▼ **A** Everyday work in Sri Lanka

	Hours per month	
	Men	**Women**
Farming	298	299
Housework	90	199
Fetching water and firewood	30	50
Worship and helping others	8	12
Total work hours	**426**	**560**
Leisure/sleep	294	160

▼ **B** Women's work

— BUT WHAT WILL WOMEN DO
IF THEY DON'T HAVE TO
CARRY WATER FOUR HOURS
A DAY?

▲ **C**

1 Use table A.
  a) Copy the following sentences, correcting those that are false.
    Men do more farm work than women.
    Women do more housework than men.
    Women have much more free time than men.
  b) Make up some sentences of your own to show the differences between men's and women's work.

2 Look at cartoon B. What answer might the women in the picture give to the man?

3 a) What two jobs is the woman in photo C doing?
  b) Give the photo your own title.

Comparing rural and urban life

We have seen that people move to cities to look for jobs and better pay. There are other good points about city life.

- Health care is better. More children die before they are one year old in rural areas than in cities.
- There are more schools. In Pakistan more women in cities can read than in rural areas.

But housing, health, and education are still poor for many city migrants.

- **Squatter settlements** in Freetown, Sierra Leone, have no clean water or sewers. One in four children dies before the age of one.
- Poor people cannot collect wood from forests. They must buy expensive firewood.

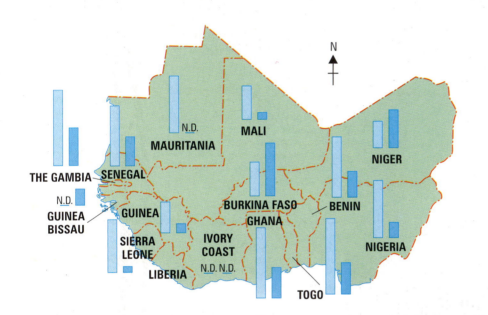

N

◄ **D** This shows the percentage of people who can get clean water in West Africa

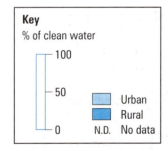

Key
% of clean water

100

50

0

Urban

Rural

N.D. No data

Factfile: Life in the Indian countryside

- Rural women spend more than seven hours a day fetching wood and water.
- Rural women breathe in dangerous amounts of wood smoke from their cooking fires. This is bad for their health.
- When wood cannot be found, rural women burn cow dung. This makes more air pollution than wood. It is better to use cow dung as manure on the farm.

4 Use this unit to fill in the table below.

Moving to the city	Good points	Bad points
Work		
Health		
Education		
Water		
Other needs		

5 Use map D. What percentage of people in Nigeria can get clean water in:

a) rural areas

b) urban areas.

c) How many West African countries have more clean water in the cities than in rural areas?

How can life be improved in rural areas?

The Tarbela Dam in North West Pakistan generates hydro-electricity. The electricity is used by factories in nearby Islamabad. But the dam has not helped local people.

- Local people still have no electricity.
- The reservoir flooded many valley roads.
- Reservoir water is not clean enough to drink. Dirty drinking water causes illness amongst local people.

▼ **B** North West Pakistan

PAKISTAN

N

km
0   100

Key
- Over 3000m
- 1000–3000m
- 500–1000m
- 0–500m

AFGHANISTAN

N.W. FRONTIER PROVINCE

Indus

JAMMU AND KASHMIR

Lake Tarbela

Kabul

Peshawar

Islamabad

Rawalpindi

PAKISTAN

INDIA

Mangla

Indus

Dam

Jhelum

Chenab

▼ **A** The women of Kalinger

1 a) On what river is Lake Tarbela?
  b) How far is Lake Tarbela from Islamabad, the capital of Pakistan?

2 Name one way in which the Tarbela Dam has affected local people.

3 Who do you think has gained from the dam?

A new water supply for Kalinger?

Kalinger village has no water supply. Women fetch clean water from springs and streams up in the hills. Women and girls carry the water in pots on their heads. Each trip takes two hours.

The women want a storage tank to hold water piped from a spring. Water could then be piped to homes, or standpipes. Action Aid is a charity that helps with such projects. Photo D shows a village in Pakistan that now has a fresh water supply.

▼ **C People in Kalinger talk about the need for a new water supply**

4 Read what the villagers in picture C have to say.
  a) List the reasons for a storage tank in the village.
  b) What reasons do the men give for not fetching water?
  c) Who do you agree with, the men or the women? Give your reasons.

5 Imagine that you live in a similar village and spend hours carrying water every day. What arguments would you give to someone who did not want a water tank in your village?

Women are happy to walk a long way for water. It lets them meet and chat to friends.

I'd like water piped to my home. People will argue about taking turns if we have just a standpipe.

I wish I could spend more time looking after my children instead of fetching water.

I never fetch water. That is only women's work. But I'd help if my wife was sick.

We are worn out by this hard work. Water pots are so heavy they rub away the hair on our heads.

◄ **D** This fresh water supply saves hours of hard work

Improving rural life in Sri Lanka

Tea used to be grown near Kandy in Sri Lanka. In the 1970s the **plantations**, or large tea farms, were sold and the tea bushes sold for firewood. New crops would not grow in the worn out soil without expensive **fertilizers**. People had to carry water from the streams by hand.

Now farmers are trying **organic farming**. This means that they do not use chemical fertilizers or pesticides. They hope it will earn money and stop people from moving away to the capital city, Colombo.

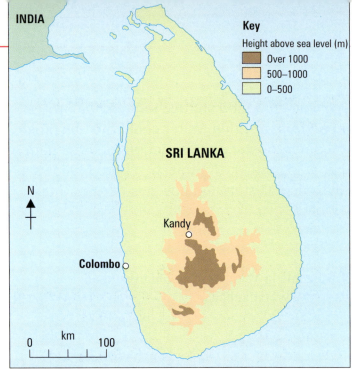

▲ A The organic farm is in Kandy, Sri Lanka

▶ B Organic farming in Kandy

Can organic farming help Sri Lanka's villages?

Christian Aid helps to pay for an organic farming project near Kandy. It needs to be:

- cheap and easy for local people to use
- safe for the environment.

How the project works

1 A small farm tries organic methods of farming. Workers then show these ideas to other farmers. They use:
    - cow dung, not chemicals, as fertilizers for tea plants
    - oil from a local seed, called *neem*, to kill plant pests
    - crushed *neem* as a compost.
2 Villagers use a van to take their vegetables to sell in the market. Money from selling the vegetables is used to run the van, and any money left over is profit for the farmers.
3 Bio-digesters make gas from cow dung and are used for heating and cooking.
4 New cooking stoves which make less smoke are being used in people's homes.

▲ **D** Making compost

▼ **C** Using a bio-digester

1 Explain two problems that farmers had before the project started.

2 Explain two organic farming methods being used by the project. What makes each method:
   a) cheap   **b)** safe for the environment?

3 Work in pairs. Imagine that one of you is working on the Kandy project. The other is a local farmer who wants to know how he could improve his farming. Tape your discussion.

4 Design a poster to show local farmers about organic farming methods. Some people may not be able to read so you will need to use pictures.

Improving health and education

There are many projects in Sri Lanka that try to improve life for rural people. Graph A shows that **life expectancy** in Sri Lanka has doubled since 1920. This means people can now expect to live longer.

The problem of malaria

Malaria is a common disease in tropical countries. The malaria parasite lives in human blood. It is carried from person to person by the mosquito. It causes a disease which can kill a young or weak person. Malaria was a major cause of death in Sri Lanka. Diagram B shows how the disease is spread.

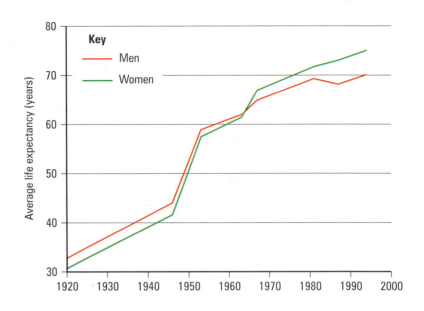

▼ **A** Life expectancy in Sri Lanka

1 What was the life expectancy for men and women in:
a) 1920
b) 1990?

2 When did women start living longer than men?

▶ **B**
How malaria is spread

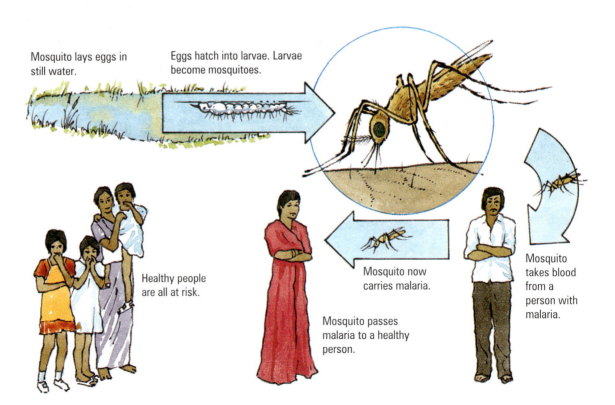

Mosquito lays eggs in still water.

Eggs hatch into larvae. Larvae become mosquitoes.

Healthy people are all at risk.

Mosquito now carries malaria.

Mosquito passes malaria to a healthy person.

Mosquito takes blood from a person with malaria.

Fighting malaria

In 1946 the government of Sri Lanka tried to wipe out the malaria mosquito. Insecticide was sprayed on still water to kill the larvae. Far fewer people die from malaria, but malaria is still a problem in some areas. Health workers show villagers how to get rid of mosquitoes.

Education in rural development

Voluntary groups in Sri Lanka help to teach people about health and the environment. The Lanka Mahila Samithi (LMS) is a group of village women who help rural people.
  They explain:
- why toilets should be kept clean and free from flies
- how to turn waste into compost for use as a fertilizer
- how to get a healthy diet.

▼ **C** Two women discussing the LMS project

The LMS helped us a lot. Now we can mend broken handpumps. We don't need our husbands to do it.

I thought boiled water was no good. I've learnt boiling water kills the germs which cause disease.

3 Why is it important for people in Sri Lanka to understand how mosquitoes spread malaria?

4 Design a poster that could be used by the LMS to teach villagers about one of the health issues.

5 Use the information in this unit to write about improving life in rural areas. Choose one of the following topics:
- health
- water
- farming.
You may add maps and pictures.

Review

Rural development is important because:
- most people in Asia and Africa live in rural areas
- rural life is often harder than city life.

The best developments in rural areas:
- use local people
- are cheap and easy to run.

4 Working in the city

We have seen that people move to the cities to find work.
- What kind of work is found in different cities?
- How is work changing?

We will look at two very different cities: Stoke-on-Trent in the UK, and Hong Kong in South East Asia.

Work in Stoke-on-Trent

The pottery industry of Stoke-on-Trent is world famous. The inner city was once full of small pottery firms. Locals called the city 'Smoke-on-Stench' because of coal smoke from the pottery kilns. This air pollution was unhealthy and turned buildings black. Now only a few large pottery firms are left.

▼ **B** Hand work in a pottery is often highly skilled

Change in the city

Graph C shows that work in Stoke is changing. There are fewer factories, such as potteries, that make things. We say there is less **manufacturing industry**. Instead there are more jobs that give a **service**, such as in hotels, shops and schools.

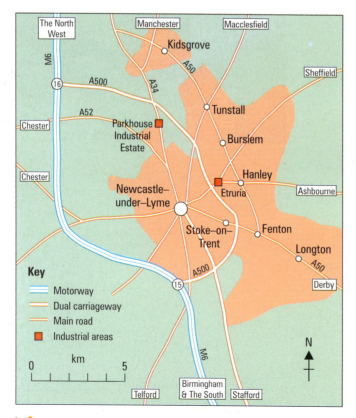

The North West
Manchester
Macclesfield
Kidsgrove
M6
A50
Sheffield
16
A500
A34
A52
Chester
Parkhouse Industrial Estate
Tunstall
Chester
Burslem
Hanley
Newcastle-under-Lyme
Etruria
Ashbourne
Stoke-on-Trent
Fenton
Longton
A50
A500
15
Derby
Key
Motorway
Dual carriageway
Main road
Industrial areas
0 km 5
N
M6
Telford
Birmingham & The South
Stafford

▲ **A** Stoke-on-Trent and Newcastle-under-Lyme

▼ **C** **How work in Stoke has changed**

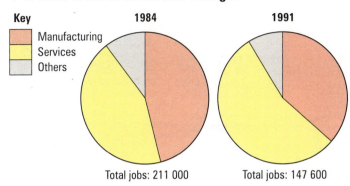

Key
- Manufacturing
- Services
- Others

1984   1991

Total jobs: 211 000   Total jobs: 147 600

Modern factories

Stoke is **accessible** or easy to reach. It has new factories in new industrial areas. Photo D shows one of these new industrial estates. The large factory at the top of the photo is a modern brick factory. It employs highly skilled people to work hi-tech equipment such as computerized electric kilns.

1 Write a list of different jobs in:
  a) manufacturing (making things)
  b) service (providing people with things they need).
  Use the jobs mentioned on these pages, and think of more of your own.

2 Use chart C. Copy the sentences below, choosing the right words.
  a) In 1984, most jobs in Stoke were in *services/manufacturing*.
  b) By 1991 there were *fewer/more* jobs than before, and the greater percentage was in *services/manufacturing*.

3 Use map A.
  a) Describe the location of Parkhouse Industrial Estate.
  b) Explain how you could get there from Birmingham.

▶ **D** **The Parkhouse Industrial Estate has one of the most modern brick factories in Europe**

Industrial change in the city

What happens when an industry closes?
Etruria was a district in the centre of
Stoke-on-Trent. It had potteries, a
railway, and gas and steel works. Look
at A, B, and C to see what it used
to be like.

▶ **A** Etruria in the 1930s
by CW Brown

▼ **B** Adapted from *Inferno to Flowers*, by Elaine Bryan and Neville Fisher, 1986

Etruria by night

White-hot slag from the steelworks was poured onto the slagheaps, down the
slope. At night its glow coloured the clouds, lighting everywhere for miles.
Bright red at first, it slowly faded to a dull glow. It worried strangers but it
made local folk feel good. Travellers knew they were nearly home when they
saw the red sky of Etruria.

▼ **C** This OS map at 1:25 000 shows how land was used in Etruria in the 1960s

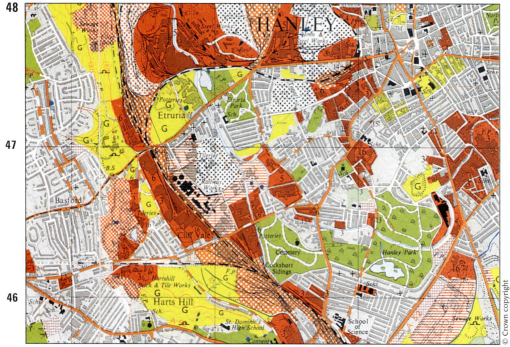

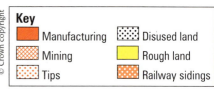

Key

▨ Manufacturing	▨ Disused land
▨ Mining	▨ Rough land
▨ Tips	▨ Railway sidings

© Crown copyright

1 Name two factories on
map C that would have
polluted or spoilt the look
of the area. Give a grid
reference for each one.

2 Look at picture A.
  a) List the activities that
  you can see.
  b) Which activities would
  cause pollution?
  c) Which activities would
  be missing, or different,
  in Etruria today?

3 Using all the information on
this page write about:
  a) the good points about
  old Etruria
  b) the bad points about old
  Etruria.

4 Would you have been glad
to live in old Etruria? Give
reasons for your answer.

Etruria today

When the British Steel factory in Etruria closed in 1979, 3000 jobs were lost. The factory site became empty. The City Council bought the land for £7.5 million. They spent £17.45 million on improving the site. The 1986 Garden Festival was held there. This helped the city in many ways:

- £8.03 million was made from ticket sales
- £12.5 million was made by builders and other companies
- visitors spent £7.2 million in local shops and hotels
- a landscaped site was left with services (roads, water, and electricity) to attract new industry.

New jobs in Etruria

Photos D and E show what the site looks like today. Some new manufacturing industries have been set up. Other jobs on the site are in service industries such as offices, shops and leisure facilities. There are around 2500 new jobs in Etruria. Many of these jobs are unskilled or part-time.

▼ **D** Leisure facilities, grid reference 871479

▼ **E** Shopping facilities, grid reference 873477

5 a) How much did it cost to improve the British Steel factory site?
b) How much money did the Garden Festival raise for the area in total?
c) Explain how holding the 1986 Garden Festival has helped Etruria today.

6 Imagine that you grew up in Etruria in the 1960s, and left in 1980 when you lost your job. Write about your return to Etruria this year, mentioning both the things that have gone and the new developments that you can see. Use map C and all the information on these pages to help you.

Hong Kong

Hong Kong is on the coast of southern China. It has a population of about 6 million. It is a world financial centre, so it has many banks. Hong Kong also manufactures and **exports** goods all over the world as you can see in table B.

Jobs in finance and banking

Hong Kong has the second largest stock market in Asia. Most of the world's top banks have branches there. One in ten jobs in Hong Kong are in banking. People in the top jobs work hard and are highly paid. Their rent and their children's education are often paid for by their company. There are also rich factory-owners and shop-owners in the city.

Less well-paid work

Not everyone in Hong Kong is rich. There are domestic helpers, factory workers, and street **hawkers**. Delia, in photo C, is one of 120 000 domestic workers in Hong Kong. Most of them come from the Philippines, leaving their families behind.

▼ **B** Hong Kong's trading partners

Country	Exports (%)
China	28
USA	27
Germany	6
Singapore	5
UK	5

Country	Imports (%)
China	38
Japan	17
Taiwan	9

▼ **A** Inside the Hong Kong and Shanghai Bank Head Office

▼ **C**

I'm a domestic helper, working for a banker. I live with the family and work about 70 hours a week. I do the cleaning and cooking, and look after the children. I miss my own children in Manila, in the Philippines. I've lived away from them for six years now. I want to go home but jobs there are badly paid. I earn as much here as a doctor gets paid in the Philippines.

Street sellers

Unemployment in Hong Kong is less than 2%. People with no regular jobs do all kinds of work. Street hawkers sell fruit, T-shirts or watches. Others deliver goods or collect materials for recycling, like the man in photo D.

This is '**informal work**'. Such workers do not get a regular wage. Often they pay no taxes and some may be breaking the law. Street traders should buy a licence, but thousands of illegal hawkers are caught and fined every year.

▼ **E** Women preparing vegetables to sell in the market

▼ **D** Collecting cardboard from the market for recycling

1 Write down one way in which a domestic worker and a wealthy bank employer are:
a) similar   **b)** different.

2 Imagine that you are Delia. Would you go home or stay? Give reasons for your answer.

3 Use table B. Show this information as a pair of divided bar graphs or a pie chart. What do your graphs tell you about Hong Kong's trading partners?

4 Look at photos A, D, and E.
a) Discuss the advantages and disadvantages of the type of work shown in photo A.
b) Discuss the advantages and disadvantages of the type of work shown in photos D and E.
c) Explain one way in which 'informal work' is different from other work.

How are jobs changing in Hong Kong?

Hong Kong has almost no **raw materials**. It produces no natural materials like timber, oil, or metal so it imports all the materials needed for industry. It produces manufactured goods like clothing, plastics, and electronics. It then exports 80% of these goods. This means that Hong Kong's harbour and airport are amongst the busiest in the world.

▶ **A** The small ships that come from China are still unloaded by hand

▼ **B** The main urban areas of Hong Kong

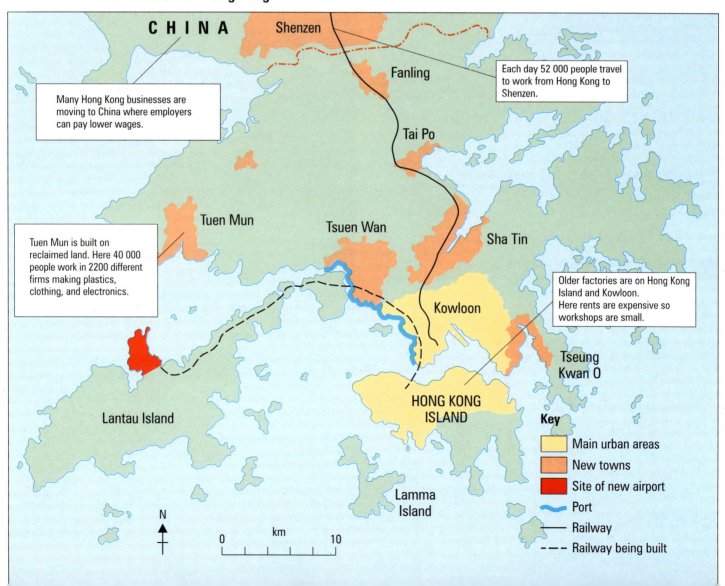

Many Hong Kong businesses are moving to China where employers can pay lower wages.

Each day 52 000 people travel to work from Hong Kong to Shenzen.

Tuen Mun is built on reclaimed land. Here 40 000 people work in 2200 different firms making plastics, clothing, and electronics.

Older factories are on Hong Kong Island and Kowloon. Here rents are expensive so workshops are small.

CHINA
Shenzen
Fanling
Tai Po
Tuen Mun
Tsuen Wan
Sha Tin
Kowloon
Tseung Kwan O
HONG KONG ISLAND
Lantau Island
Lamma Island

N

0   km   10

Key
- Main urban areas
- New towns
- Site of new airport
- Port
- Railway
- Railway being built

Manufacturing

The back streets of Hong Kong are full of hundreds of small workshops mixed in with shops and street markets. Families live in the tower blocks above. This makes it noisy and crowded but workers do not have far to go to work. Workshops produce anything from T-shirts to parts for air-conditioners, like the man in photo C. The Hong Kong government encourages these small firms. More than 88% of manufacturing firms are small and employ less than twenty people.

Industrial change in Hong Kong

In the last five years, jobs have been lost in manufacturing. Some companies have moved to China where workers are paid less. Graph D shows job losses in the clothing industry which was once Hong Kong's biggest employer. Photo E shows another reason for job losses: the use of new technology.

1 How many people were employed in the clothing industry in
a) 1983 **b)** 1993?
c) How many jobs have been lost since 1983?

2 Use map B. Name an area with:
a) modern factories **b)** older factories.

3 a) Use this unit to fill in the table below.

Manufacturing in Hong Kong and Stoke

Factories	Hong Kong	Factories in Stoke
Size		
Products		
Location		

b) How are factories in these two places similar?
c) How are they different?

▼ **C** A metalworker shapes part of an air-conditioner outside his small workshop

▼ **E** Designing sails using computers

▼ **D** The loss of jobs in the clothing industry

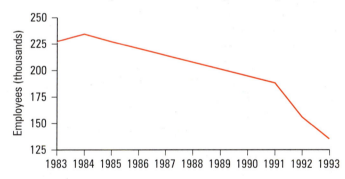

Self-help in the city

What happens if you are unemployed or only have a part-time job in the city? What other kinds of work could you do?

Work in the *favelas* of Rio de Janeiro

The population of Rio de Janeiro in Brazil is 9.6 million. About 3 million people live in *favelas* (**shanty towns**). Some of these people have regular paid jobs. Others do informal work, like street selling. In their free time, people get together to improve the *favela*. They help each other to improve homes, footpaths and steps through the town. They also work on community buildings in the *favela*, as can be seen in photo A.

Rio de Janeiro
BRAZIL

▲ **A People give up free time and work for no pay to help the *favela***

1 Use graph B. Make a list of countries where more people live in shanty town housing than in proper housing.

2 Explain how people are improving the *favela* for themselves.

Cities in **developing countries** often grow very fast. It is hard to provide all the housing and services they need. So some people who move there build shanty towns. They may have no electricity, sewage system or water supply, but the people who live there are important to the city.

Graph B shows that, in some cities, more people live in shanties than in proper houses.

▼ **B The percentage of people living in shanty towns in the developing world**

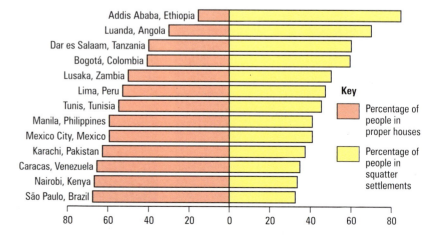

Self-build projects in the UK

In the UK, 25 000 people are building their own homes. Self-build projects help young, unemployed people to learn new skills such as plumbing, joinery, and electrical skills. When they finish building, they have a home which they can rent cheaply. Their new skills also give them a better chance of getting a job.

▲ **C** Working on a self-build project

3 a) What similarities are there between the volunteers in the *favela* and the people in the UK self-build project?

b) In what ways are they different?

Building a home and a future

Nine unemployed young men and women are on a self-build project in Maltby, Yorkshire. They were given a 10-week course in brickwork and joinery. While they are building their homes they earn an extra benefit of £10 a week. When they are finished, they will be able to rent the home they built cheaply. They also hope to pass NVQ exams as a result of their new skills.

▲ **D** Extract adapted from *The Times*, 2 November 1994

Review

- Cities offer many kinds of work.
- Factory and service workers are paid regular wages.
- 'Informal' workers, such as street hawkers, do not earn a regular weekly wage. Often they pay no tax.
- Some people work for no pay.

4 Do you think the self-help projects are a good idea? Give your reasons.

5 List the different jobs studied in this unit. Fit them into the following groups:
- manufacturing
- service industries
- informal work
- unpaid work.

5 Kenya

Kenya, in East Africa, is a developing country. To see how it is changing we will look at the following questions.

- What is Kenya's environment like?
- Why do tourists visit Kenya?
- How does tourism affect Kenya?
- What is life like in rural and urban areas?

▼ **A** Kenya's natural environment

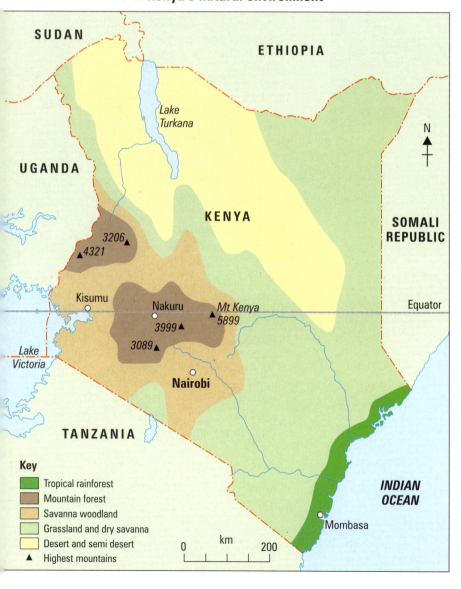

Key
- Tropical rainforest
- Mountain forest
- Savanna woodland
- Grassland and dry savanna
- Desert and semi desert
- ▲ Highest mountains

0 km 200

Kenya's natural environment

Tropical rainforests grow along Kenya's coastline. This area is very green, hot and wet. The rainforest has been cleared in places to make space to grow bananas, coconuts and pineapples.

Factfile: Kenya

- Kenya has the highest **birth rate** in the world.
- Nearly half of the population is aged less than fifteen.
- Mount Kenya is on the Equator. It is over 5000m, so high that its peak is covered in snow.
- The oldest human bones ever discovered were found in Kenya.

1 a) Use map A. Make a list of Kenya's environments. Put them in order of size, starting with the largest areas.

b) Use the scale to measure the length of Kenya's rainforest.

On safari

Away from the coast, Kenya is very dry. Crops do not grow well on the dry grasslands or **savanna**. Lake Turkana, in the north, is surrounded by desert. The south-west has more rain so the landscape is green, with many trees. Most of the crops are grown here.

More and more tourists visit Kenya each year. They come to see its wildlife and different landscapes. 8% of Kenya's land has been made into National Parks to protect the wildlife. In the Maasai Mara you can watch wildlife from a safari bus or a hot-air balloon. Buses take visitors close to the animals but they can upset them, and damage the landscape. Hot-air balloons do not harm the landscape but they frighten some animals.

▲ C Rainforest on Kenya's coast

▶ D Tourism gives Kenya a large part of its income

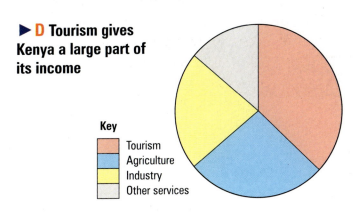

Key

■ Tourism
■ Agriculture
■ Industry
■ Other services

▼ B A hot-air balloon over the savanna in the Maasai Mara

2 Look at photos B and C.
   a) List the differences between the trees and plants.
   b) What can you tell about differences in the climates?
   c) Which photo shows a drier climate?

3 Look at pie chart D. What percentage of Kenya's income comes from tourism?

4 a) Give one reason why tourists might wish to visit Kenya.

   b) Imagine that you are visiting the Maasai Mara in Kenya. Would you rather watch the wildlife from a safari bus or a hot-air balloon? Give reasons for your choice.

Kenya's coast

▲ **A** Watamu Beach, Malindi

Tourists come to enjoy Kenya's beaches as well as its wildlife. Kenya's coastline is just south of the Equator so there is sunshine and high temperatures all year round. The tropical climate and beautiful beaches bring many visitors from Europe and the USA. The Kenyan coast is a fast-growing tourist area.

▼ **B** Mombasa's climate

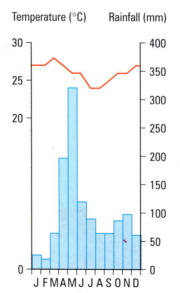

Temperature (°C)   Rainfall (mm)

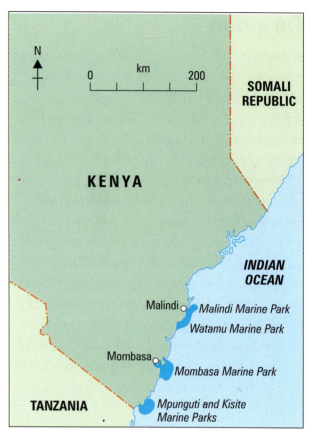

▲ **C** The coastline of Kenya

Malindi – heaven on earth?

From Malindi village to Watamu there are wonderful, sandy beaches with dunes and casuarina trees. Beautiful potato staghorn and mushroom coral grow in the warm seas. The coral reef off Malindi is now a marine reserve.

▲ **D** Holidays in Malindi

1 Why do tourists visit Kenya's coast? Give three reasons.

The coral reef

There is a coral reef one kilometre from the Kenyan coast. It grows in the warm, shallow waters. It has taken millions of years to grow.

The coral reef is enjoyed in many different ways:

- scuba divers and snorkellers look at the wildlife
- people wind-surf in the quiet waters behind the reef
- big-game fishing boats cross the reef to fish in the Indian Ocean. They catch bonito, kingfish, barracuda and marlin.

Damage to the reef

The coral reef is in danger. It is being destroyed by the thousands of visitors to the area. Much of the coral has died already and the reef is broken in places. At low tide, visitors in glass-bottomed boats break off coral or take living shells. Sewage from hotels also damages the coral. Tourists are now kept to areas where the coral is already damaged, to save the unspoilt parts of the reef.

▲ **F** The coral reef off the coast of Kenya

2 List the ways in which tourists are damaging the coral reef.

3 What do you think could happen to the tourist industry on the coast if the reef was destroyed?

4 Produce a leaflet on Kenya using pictures, maps and diagrams. Show *either* places to visit and activities for tourists, *or* the dangers to Kenya's coast.

▼ **E** The impact of tourism on the coral reef

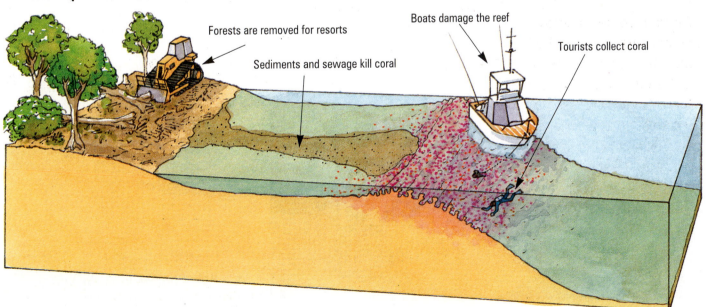

Forests are removed for resorts

Sediments and sewage kill coral

Boats damage the reef

Tourists collect coral

Work in Kenya

Tourism brings in a lot of money for Kenya, but does not provide many jobs. Most Kenyans live and work in rural areas.

Rural life

In most of Africa, women do the hard work in the villages. Many hours are spent:
- fetching water
- looking after crops
- collecting wood.

Wood is important in rural areas for cooking fires, building houses, for light, and even for toothbrushes.

Photo A shows the inside of a rural home called an *ola*. It is a one-roomed house made of timber and thatch. Ware Kiya's *ola* has been burnt down in a cooking accident. She would like to live in a stone house with a bathroom. Her daughter wants a quiet room for doing her school work.

▼ **A** Cooking in an *ola*

1 Look carefully at photo A.
   a) List the kitchen equipment you can see and explain its use.
   b) How would cooking a meal in an *ola* be similar, or different, to preparing a meal in your home?

2 Look at photo C. Describe the load that the women are carrying. You may wish to use some of the words below.

   light   tiring   heavy
   awkward   balance

3 Use bar graph B.

   a) Give the percentage of income spent by Kenyan and UK families on:
      (i) food
      (ii) health
      (iii) housing and fuel.
   b) Write about the differences you see.

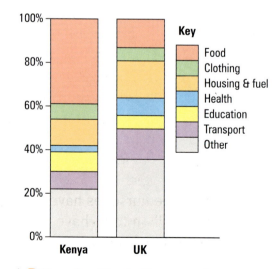

Key
- Food
- Clothing
- Housing & fuel
- Health
- Education
- Transport
- Other

▲ **B** How families in Kenya and the UK spend their money

◀ **C**
Women returning home with firewood

The need for firewood

People who live in rural areas use huge amounts of firewood. Cutting down many trees is called **deforestation**. Wangari Maathai, a Kenyan professor, was worried by the number of trees being cut down. She saw that when the trees have gone the land becomes useless. The land dries out and crops will not grow. Wangari asked women to help because they not only use wood for cooking, but they also farm the land. Working with Kenyan women, she set up a tree-planting project and taught people about the problems of deforestation. Now 50 000 women are part of the project. Tree nurseries have been set up and more than 7 million trees have been planted. More areas will be replanted in the next five years.

▼ **D** Kenya's firewood problem

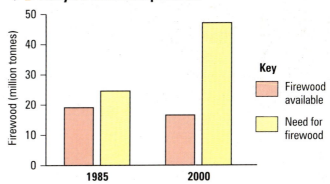

Key
■ Firewood available
■ Need for firewood

4 a) Give one reason for deforestation in Kenya.
b) What will be the effect of deforestation?
c) Use graph D to describe what will happen to the need for firewood by the year 2000.
d) Why are women more affected by deforestation than men?
e) How will Wangari Maathai's project help with the problem of deforestation?

Farming in Kenya

◀ **A** A Kenyan woman looks after her goats

A village in the savanna is made up of homesteads. Each homestead has a number of one-roomed houses and an area for keeping goats and cattle. Cattle must be kept safe from leopards, lions and hyenas at night. Plan B shows the layout of a homestead.

The land is too dry to grow crops. Milk is the main food. Cattle are kept for milk and goats for meat. The animals are moved from place to place to graze. This means that the vegetation is not destroyed. Goats eat anything, so they are stopped from eating small trees and bushes which people need for firewood.

Crops are grown in the wetter parts of the country. People in Kenya eat maize, wheat, rice and vegetables. Crops such as coffee and tea are grown for export.

▼ **B** A homestead in a Maasai village

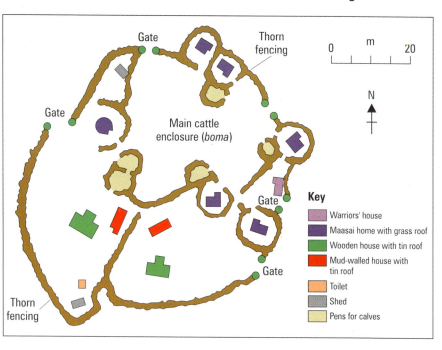

Gate

Thorn fencing

Main cattle enclosure (*boma*)

Gate

Gate

Gate

Thorn fencing

Key
- Warriors' house
- Maasai home with grass roof
- Wooden house with tin roof
- Mud-walled house with tin roof
- Toilet
- Shed
- Pens for calves

1 Copy the sentences below. Fill in the gaps using diagram B.
A Maasai home is surrounded by .... It has many .... or timber houses with grass or .... roofs. .... are kept in enclosures near the houses.

Moving to the town

in 1994 75% of Kenya's population lived in rural areas. But more and more people are moving to the cities. The city populations are growing quickly, as graph C shows.

Men who cannot earn enough money from farming move to the city to find work. Women are left in the villages to look after the land, animals and children. Some men never come back or send money to their families.

▼ **C** Kenya's growing urban population

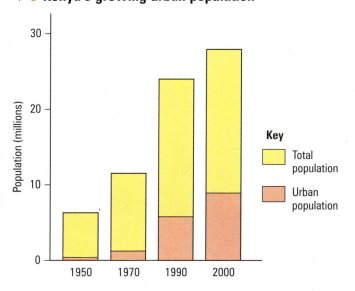

Key
Total population
Urban population

Women leaving the villages

Kenyan women have also had to leave their villages. In Kenya women work the land but men own it. When a husband dies, the wife cannot keep his land. If there is no work in the village she is forced to move to the town to find a job. Maria Mathai ran her husband's farm near Mount Kenya while he worked away from the village. When he died the village chief told her she could not stay. Maria and her four daughters had to leave.

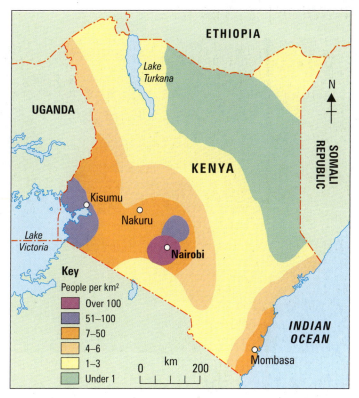

Key
People per km²
- Over 100
- 51–100
- 7–50
- 4–6
- 1–3
- Under 1

▲ **D** Population density in Kenya

Improving rural life

The Kenyan government has set up projects to improve life in rural areas so that fewer people will move to the cities. One project in Kibwezi village gives goat milk to children. A bee-keeping project makes honey to sell locally and abroad. Fish and rabbit farming are also being tried.

2 Use map D.
  a) Which parts of Kenya have the least people?
  b) Use map A on page 48 to give a reason.

3 a) Why do men move to the towns?
  b) How can this affect their families?
  c) What different reasons might women have for moving to a town?

4 How can people be helped to stay in their villages?

◀ **A**
Nairobi from Uhuru Park

Life in the city

Men and women move to cities looking for a better life. But is life really better in the city? In fact, 70% of Nairobi's 2 million people are poor. Many of them live in shanty towns. Many people have poorly paid jobs and most of their money is spent on food. Food prices are rising faster than the wages of poor people.

▲ **B** Many materials are used to build simple housing in a shanty town

1 a) Use photo B. List the different materials used to build the houses.

b) Imagine that you had to make your own home from whatever materials you could find. List the things you might use and the problems you might have.

2 Describe what it might be like to live in the shanty town in the rainy season.

3 Use photo A. Write a sentence to describe Nairobi.

◀ **C**

These children of Kariobangi built their go-kart from recycled materials. They recycle rubbish to make toys. They use bicycle wheels as hoops. Toy trucks are made from washing powder tins and bottle tops. Anything that is not used will be eaten by Kariobangi's goats!

Recycling for a living

Kariobangi is a shanty town on the outskirts of Nairobi. It is home to 60 000 people. Some of these people work in the city but many earn money in Kariobangi itself. People sell basic goods and sweets, or crafts made in small workshops. Kariobangi is next to Nairobi's rubbish tip. So most people use the rubbish to make things to sell.

Factfile: Recycling

People find things on the rubbish tip to resell, repair or make into new goods.

- Oil lamps are made from tins.
- Bracelets are made from plastic and wire strips.
- Sandals are made from tyres.
- Cooking pots are made from scrap metal.
- Plastic bottles are used for carrying water.
- Corn cobs become bottle stoppers.

4 Look at photo C. List the items that have been reused to make the go-kart.

5 a) List the items that are recycled in Kariobangi.
b) Which of these items are recycled in your household?
c) What happens to these items?

6 Choose an item that you regularly throw away, and think of a new use for it. Draw pictures or diagrams to explain how it could be recycled.

7 The children in photo C may have been born in a savanna village. Give reasons why they might be glad to live in Kariobangi. Give reasons why they might wish to live in a village in Kenya.

Kenya – a modern trading country

Kenya earns more money from its industries than other East African countries. It produces cloth, shoes, and food products such as coffee and flour. More than 60% of Kenya's industry is owned by companies which have offices in Nairobi but are based in other countries. The city has good roads and an international airport.

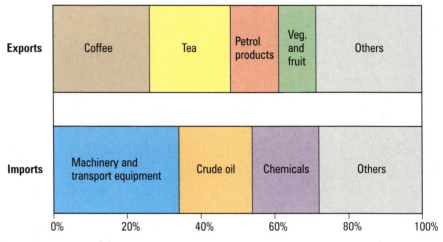

▼ **A** Kenya's imports and exports

▼ **B** Wealth created by industry

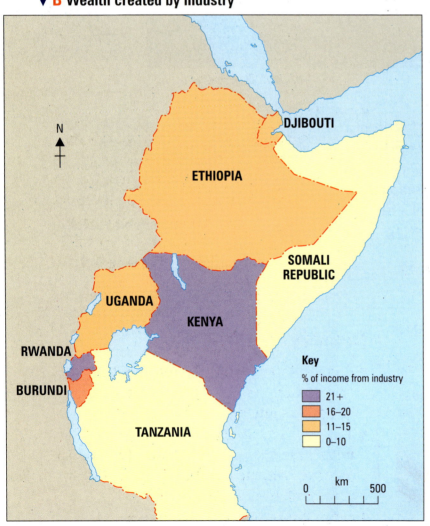

Key
% of income from industry
- 21+
- 16–20
- 11–15
- 0–10

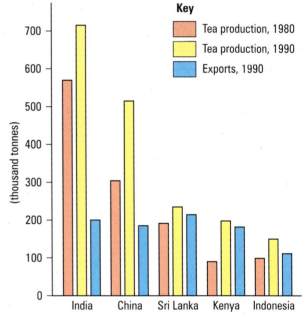

Key
- Tea production, 1980
- Tea production, 1990
- Exports, 1990

▲ **C** World tea producers and exporters

Country	Tea production		Exports
	1980	1990	1990
Turkey	96	140	28
Bangladesh	40	45	27
Malawi	30	43	39

▲ **D** Tea production and exports (in thousands of tonnes)

▲ **E Picking tea in Kenya**

▲ **F Tea growing areas**

1 Use graph A to copy and complete the following sentences.
   Kenya's largest export is .... Tea comes second with .... % of all exports. Kenya's biggest import is .... Crude oil makes .... % of all imports.

2 What does map B tell you about the success of Kenya's industry compared to its neighbours?

3 Use graph C.
   a) Did tea production increase or decrease between 1980 and 1990?
   b) Name two countries that exported most of their crop in 1990?

4 a) Use table D. Draw a bar graph (like the one in C) for either Turkey, Bangladesh or Malawi.
   b) Write a sentence to explain how tea production in your chosen country compares with Kenya.

Tea in Kenya

The tea grown in Kenya is of very high quality. Most of it is exported and demand for it is increasing. In 1990 tea exports earned US $273 million. In 1991, 200 000 tonnes were produced. A huge government project is now under way to increase the amount of tea grown to 300 000 tonnes by the end of this century.

Review

- Tourism earns money for Kenya but the environment needs to be protected from its harmful effects.
- Most Kenyans live in rural areas. Many people are moving to the cities. Projects to improve rural life may help people to stay in their villages.
- Kenya trades with other countries.

6 Making the most of the weather

We will look at the following questions.
● How and why does the weather affect us?
● How do people cope with the weather?
● What is the difference between weather and climate?

Why is weather important?

Weather is made up of sunshine, wind, rain and temperature. We are affected by the weather every day. Our activities, the clothes we wear, even where we would like to go on holiday, are all affected by the weather. The tennis match in photo B, for example, was relying on dry weather.

Health risks from the cold

We need warmth to stay healthy. Our bodies cannot keep themselves warm at temperatures below 6°. People can die from a condition called hypothermia. Elderly people are often affected because they are less active. Young babies are also at risk because the system which controls their body temperature is not yet developed.

1 Work in pairs.
  a) Discuss yesterday's weather. Think about temperature, rainfall, wind and sunshine.
  b) Describe how you were affected by the weather. Think about what you wore and what you did.
  c) Suggest an event that would not be affected by the weather.

2 Write down ways that the following are affected by weather:
  a) farmers
  b) motorway traffic
  c) elderly people.

◄ A Endangered by the cold

◄ B
Some sports need dry weather. Rain has stopped this tennis match at Wimbledon

Changes in the weather

When the weather changes it can cause problems. Weather forecasts tell us how the weather may change. They help us to prepare for problems caused by the weather.

Photo E shows road sensors. These sensors measure the temperature of the air and the dampness of the road. This information tells the highways department when to send out gritters and snow ploughs.

▼ **E** Remote snow and ice sensor

▼ **C** Road signs warn about weather hazards

FLOOD

FOG

▼ **D** A snow plough helps with winter weather

3 Explain how the following weather conditions can affect a journey by car:
  a) high winds
  b) fog
  c) snow
  d) bright sunshine.

4 Design a road sign to warn people about these weather hazards:
  a) a snow storm
  b) fog
  c) heavy rain.

5 What problems for drivers can be predicted using the sensors?

6 Imagine that the car you are travelling in becomes stuck in heavy snow. Make a list of things you should and should not do.

People can affect the weather

The weather is affected by towns and cities. Buildings and roads soak up the sun's energy. They send out heat, warming the air around them. For this reason the centre of a city is often warmer than the outskirts. This effect is called an **urban heat island**.

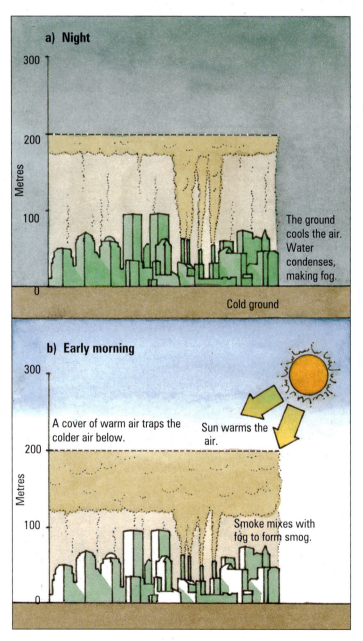

▲ **A** How smog forms in winter

Urban climate and pollution

Heating, exhaust fumes and industry can change the air we breathe.

- **Smog** is caused when cold damp air mixes with air pollution. People with breathing difficulties find smog makes them worse. Look at diagram A to see how smog is formed.
- Car fumes build up in city streets on still, sunny days. Fumes are trapped and, with no wind, new fresh air cannot be brought in. Car exhausts react with sunlight to make ozone. This gas is painful to the eyes, nose, throat and lungs. Ozone levels were high in London in 1994.

Smog, I see no smog

We know that air pollution in towns gets worse on still, sunny days. We also know this affects people with asthma and chest problems. Yet we still use our cars and lorries, knowing that they are part of the problem.

We cannot say we don't understand the problem of smog. The whole country monitors air pollution. There is a pollution forecasting service that anyone can use. Newspapers and television even warn when poor **air quality** is expected.

▲ **B** Adapted from *The Independent*, 14 July 1994

1 Copy the sentences below. Use diagram B to help fill in the gaps.
Fog forms at .... when the air is cooled by the cold ground below and water vapour .... In the early morning the sun .... the air above, trapping the cooler .... below. The fog mixes with .... to form ....

The smog problem in sunny cities

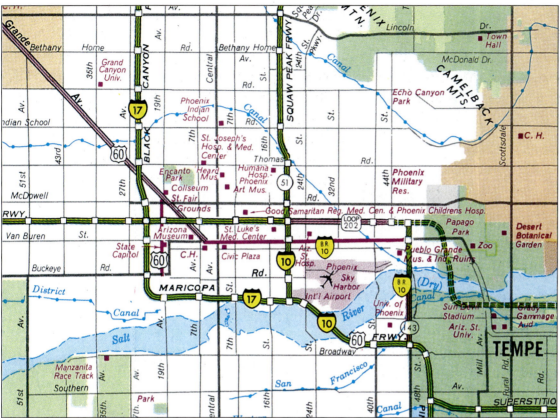

Phoenix, USA

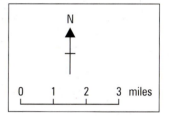

◀ **C Street map of Phoenix**

▲ **D This photo of Phoenix was taken from the air**

Phoenix is built within a huge, sunny valley in the desert state of Arizona, USA. The city was built for cars. Main roads spread 80km from the city centre to the suburbs. Commuters driving to and from work cause pollution. The pollution is trapped in the valley and reacts with the sunlight to make smog. New laws may be used to cut down the high levels of pollution.

2 How does air pollution affect people's health?

3 Read article B. Suggest one way to cut down air pollution in towns and cities.

4 a) How might life be better in Phoenix if fewer cars were used?

b) Discuss why people in Phoenix may want to carry on using their cars.

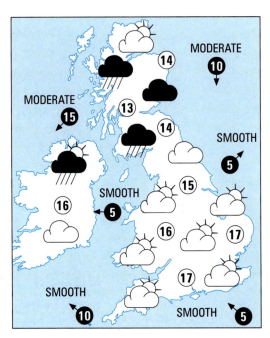

▲ **A** Weather forecast, 15 October 1994

Weather and climate

The *climate* of an area is its average weather over many years. Different parts of the UK have slightly different climates. For example Devon and Cornwall have a drier, warmer climate than the north-west of Scotland. Temperature and rainfall are important parts of climate. They are recorded to give data, which can be shown on a climate graph, such as graph B.

Weather is the day-to-day changes in temperature, rainfall and sunshine.

A warm autumn in the UK

In the UK we expect the autumn to be cold and damp. But November 1994 was the warmest for 300 years. On 15 October 1994, the south of England had temperatures of 21°C, just like a summer day. These daily changes are predicted in weather forecasts like A.

Temperature (°C)   Rainfall (mm)

▲ **B** Climate graph for Plymouth

		Jan	Feb	Mar	Apr	May	Jun	Jul	Aug	Sep	Oct	Nov	Dec
Eskdalemuir, Scotland	temp (°C)	1	2	4	6	9	11	14	13	11	8	5	3
	rain (mm)	175	112	97	97	87	108	131	120	136	149	153	162
London, England	temp (°C)	4	5	7	8	12	16	18	17	15	11	8	5
	rain (mm)	54	40	37	37	46	45	57	59	49	57	64	48
Aberystwyth, Wales	temp (°C)	4	5	6	8	11	13	15	15	13	10	8	6
	rain (mm)	97	72	60	56	65	76	99	93	108	118	111	96
Valentia, Ireland	temp (°C)	7	7	8	10	11	14	15	16	14	11	9	8
	rain (mm)	165	107	103	75	86	81	107	95	122	140	151	168

▲ **C** Climate data for places in the UK

1 Draw a climate graph for one of the places in table C. Use the same scale for temperature and rainfall as in graph B.

2 Find someone who has drawn the climate graph for a different place.
  a) Discuss similarities between the two graphs.
  b) Discuss differences between the two graphs.
  c) Write a paragraph comparing your two graphs.

A wet November in southern Europe

In November 1994 the UK had a warm autumn but in northern Italy and southern France, heavy rain caused flooding. In Piedmont, Italy, 500mm of rain fell in just 24 hours. Rivers flooded and 90 people were killed. Some died when floods swept away cars, others died in **mudslides** caused by heavy rain. In France, the damage to Nice airport may cost £4.1 million to repair.

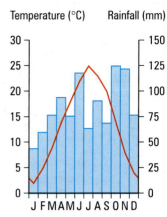

► **F Climate graph for Milan**

▲ **D The area affected by flooding**

Floods in southern Europe

When the Tanaro and Borbone rivers burst their banks, hundreds of people were trapped by the floods. Helicopters rescued them and took them to Asti. Some people said the floods were made worse because dam gates were opened in the Cuneo mountains, to prevent them bursting with the heavy rain. Officials denied that this had happened.

▲ **G Extract adapted from *The Times*, 8 November 1994**

3 Use map D.
  a) Where is the source of the River Po?
  b) In which direction does it flow?

4 500mm of rain fell in 24 hours in November 1994. Use climate graph F to work out how much more rain fell than in an average November.

5 List the different ways the weather caused damage in Europe in November 1994.

6 Find Pavia on map D. What do you notice that could explain why Pavia was badly affected by the floods?

7 Explain in your own words what is meant by:
  a) weather
  b) climate.

▲ **E A woman next to her ruined house**

Using the weather to make electricity

We have used wind power for thousands of years to sail boats, to pump water, and to power mills that process food. Wind energy is now being used to generate electricity. The oil, gas and coal that we use to make electricity are being used up. We need other alternative types of energy that will not run out. Wind energy is an example of a **renewable resource**: it is a resource that will not run out.

Factfile: Alternative energy sources

Alternative energy sources should:
- be renewable
- produce little or no pollution or waste
- make little noise, or spoil the look of a place
- not harm wildlife or the land.

▲ **B** **A modern wind farm**

Wind turbines are an alternative energy source. The best sites are the windiest ones (see map A). Wind farms are groups of wind turbines which generate electricity. They work best when built in windy places. Delabole wind farm in North Cornwall began in 1991. It has ten turbines, and was the first wind farm in the UK.

1 Use map A and an atlas.
  a) Name five of the windiest places.
  b) What do you notice about the location of the windiest areas?

2 a) Using an atlas, name a national park in a windy area.
  b) Do you think it would be good idea to build a wind farm there? Give reasons for your answer.

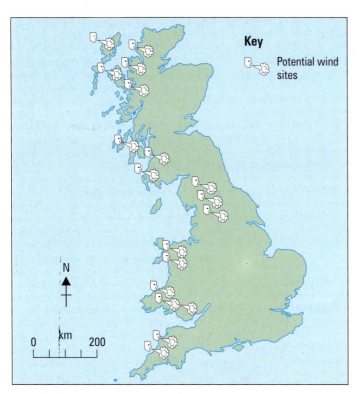

Key

🪶 Potential wind sites

N

0   km   200

▲ **A** **The windiest parts of Great Britain**

Are wind farms a good idea?

Not everyone agrees that wind farms are a good idea. A wind farm was planned in Cemmaes, in Wales. The letters in C were written to the District Council – 110 people liked the idea, but 35 were not pleased.

▼ **C** Extracts from letters sent to Montgomery District Council about the planned Cemmaes Road wind farm

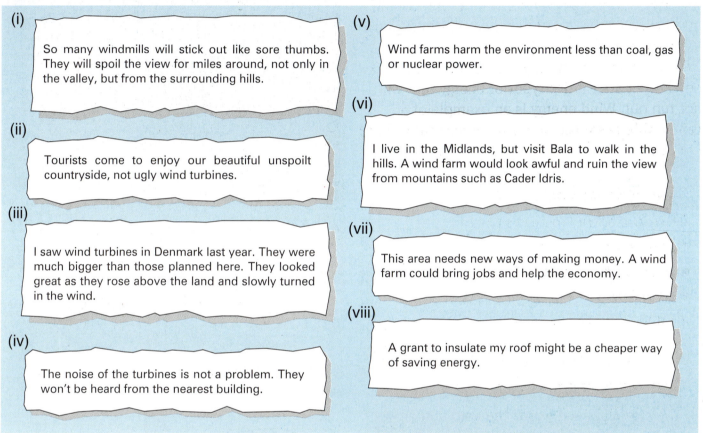

(i) So many windmills will stick out like sore thumbs. They will spoil the view for miles around, not only in the valley, but from the surrounding hills.

(ii) Tourists come to enjoy our beautiful unspoilt countryside, not ugly wind turbines.

(iii) I saw wind turbines in Denmark last year. They were much bigger than those planned here. They looked great as they rose above the land and slowly turned in the wind.

(iv) The noise of the turbines is not a problem. They won't be heard from the nearest building.

(v) Wind farms harm the environment less than coal, gas or nuclear power.

(vi) I live in the Midlands, but visit Bala to walk in the hills. A wind farm would look awful and ruin the view from mountains such as Cader Idris.

(vii) This area needs new ways of making money. A wind farm could bring jobs and help the economy.

(viii) A grant to insulate my roof might be a cheaper way of saving energy.

▼ **D** Adapted from *The Times*, 24 December 1993

Gales too strong for wind farm

Winds travelling at 160km in December broke four turbines at Cemmaes wind farm. The farm has 24 turbines. It cost at least £9 million to build and was only opened in 1992. Three of Britain's biggest wind farms have been closed because of the recent high winds.

3 Describe the wind turbines in B. Do you find them ugly or attractive? Your description may be a paragraph, or a poem. You may use the words below if you wish.

elegant   whirling   monster   looming

lonely   weird   graceful

4 Read through the letters in C.
   a) Make a list of reasons for a wind farm and a list of reasons against.
   b) If you had been a member of the District Council would you have voted for or against the wind farm? Give your reasons.

Wild weather

Some parts of the world have climates that give difficult weather conditions. One of the most powerful types of weather in the world are tropical storms. They are called **typhoons** in Asia, **hurricanes** in North America and **cyclones** in the Bay of Bengal. They can produce:

- winds up to 160kph
- heavy storms with lots of thunder and lightning
- strong winds which make huge waves. Water is pushed inland in huge waves called **storm surges**.

Storm surges cause 90% of deaths during tropical storms.

How tropical storms are formed

Tropical storms start out at sea. This is how they happen:

1 Warm, moist air rises from the ocean.
2 Cooler air rushes in. This makes violent winds and waves.
3 The warm air cools, condenses and turns to heavy rain.
4 The storm spins towards the land and grows stronger.
5 When the storm is over land it loses energy because there is no more warm water to drive the system.

Diagram B shows how a tropical storm works.

Typhoons in Hong Kong

Typhoons can hit Hong Kong between July and October. Typhoon warnings are given by radio and television to the 6 million people in Hong Kong. In 1993, Hong Kong had four warnings of very strong typhoons. One typhoon, Typhoon Dot, caused 7m deep floods. Typhoon Ira is described in article C.

▲ **A** A storm surge on the coast of Miami, Florida, 1948

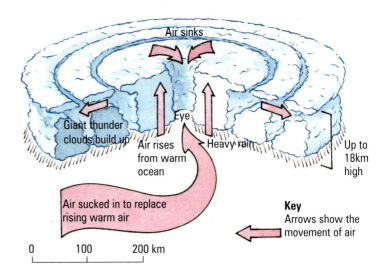

▲ **B** Cross-section through a tropical storm

Typhoon Ira hits Hong Kong

Heavy rain from Typhoon Ira caused damage in Hong Kong on 4 November, 1993. There were huge landslides on Lantau island and floods all over Tuen Mun and Yuen Long. On Cheung Chau island water supplies were cut off for four days because of burst water pipes.

▲ **C** Adapted from *Hong Kong Year Book*, 1994

◀ **D** Landslides often happen in Hong Kong after heavy rain

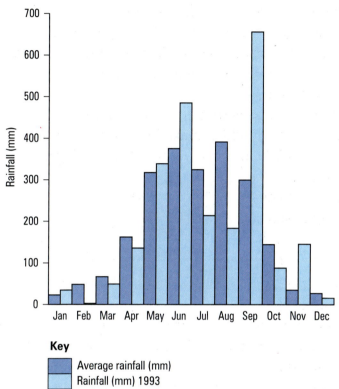

Key

■ Average rainfall (mm)
■ Rainfall (mm) 1993

▲ **E** Rainfall for 1993 compared with average rainfall in Hong Kong

1 Copy and complete the sentences below.
When warm air .... from the ocean it forms .... and heavy rain. Air is .... in, to replace the rising air. This makes high .... and .... .The storm .... towards the land. Over land the storm loses .... and dies.

2 Look at rainfall graph E.
a) How much more rain fell in November 1993 than the average for the month?
b) Suggest the month when Typhoon Dot struck Hong Kong.

3 Imagine that you are reading the news on Hong Kong radio. Read aloud or record the following:
a) a typhoon warning for 3 November 1993, just before the arrival of Typhoon Ira
b) a news report for 6 November 1993, after Typhoon Ira hit Hong Kong.

Review

- *Weather* is the daily amount of sun, wind and rain.
- *Climate* is the average weather in a place over a number of years.
- Weather and climate affect the way we live.
- We can make the best use of a place when we understand its climate. For example, we choose windy places to build wind farms.

Pressures on the Mediterranean

The Mediterranean Sea separates southern Europe and northern Africa.
- What changes in farming, industry and tourism have created problems in the area?
- How has the environment been affected?
- How can the region develop without further harm to the environment?

MEDITERRANEAN

▼ **A** Pollution in the Mediterranean

The Mediterranean Sea

The shallow Mediterranean Sea is almost surrounded by land. It meets the Atlantic Ocean at the narrow Strait of Gibraltar. It has no tide, so tourist beaches have to be swept, or they will become very dirty.

1 Use map A.
  a) Which part of the Mediterranean is the most heavily polluted, the east or the west?
  b) Which European countries might have caused this pollution?

Polluting the Mediterranean Sea

About 370 million people live in the Mediterranean region. The 200 million tourists who visit each year add to the environmental problems. Tourists, for example, use five to six times more water than local people. They also create huge amounts of waste. As much as 85% of the sewage pumped into the Mediterranean Sea is untreated.

Cleaning the beach by sweeping away dirt
▼ **B and litter**

Most pollution in the Mediterranean begins on land. It comes from waste water, chemicals washed from farms, and untreated sewage. Shipping also causes pollution. As the population grows and urban areas spread, these problems will get worse.

▲ **C Adapted from *World Bank Information Brief*, April 1994**

Waste from industry and farming

Rivers carry high levels of pollution into the Mediterranean. This pollution comes from:

- factories
- chemical fertilizers and pesticides washed off farmlands by rain
- ships carrying crude oil.

In 1991, one oil spill sent 55 million litres of oil onto the French coast. Diagram D shows how pollution is trapped in the Mediterranean.

▼ **D How pollution builds up**

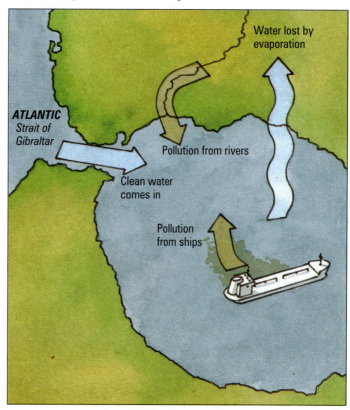

Water lost by evaporation

ATLANTIC
Strait of Gibraltar

Pollution from rivers

Clean water comes in

Pollution from ships

2 List three types of pollution that enter the sea.

3 What could happen to tourists in the Mediterranean if the beaches were not kept clean?

4 Read extract C. Does more pollution come from rivers or from ships?

5 Copy diagram D. Add a label to explain why the pollution is trapped in the Mediterranean.

People and wildlife

The millions of people who live in and visit the region make problems for the environment. Wildlife is endangered by pollution from new resorts and towns. The rare loggerhead turtle, for example, is suffering from the growth of tourism.

Every summer 2000 turtles lay eggs on Zakynthos, a small Greek island. They lay their eggs in holes in the sandy beaches. The young hatch out at night and race into the sea before they can be eaten by rats or seagulls.

▲ **B** The endangered loggerhead turtle

Tourism and turtles

Hot summers and sandy beaches attract more and more tourists to Greece. But visitors to Zakynthos are harming the turtles they come to see. During the day, tourists trample eggs buried on the beach. Tourists watching turtles at night, frighten them away so they cannot lay their eggs.

▼ **A** The eastern part of the Mediterranean region

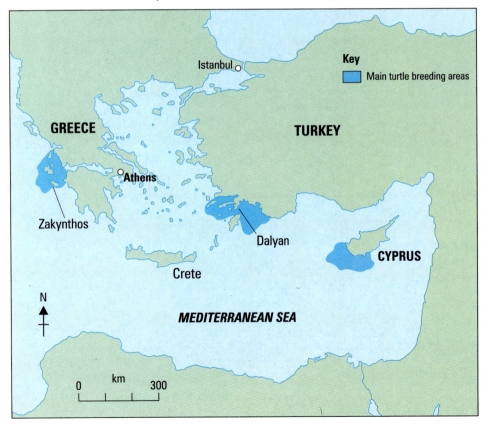

Key
■ Main turtle breeding areas

Istanbul

GREECE

TURKEY

Athens

Zakynthos

Dalyan

Crete

CYPRUS

MEDITERRANEAN SEA

N

0   km   300

Dalyan, Turkey – a place of charm and beauty

Dalyan is a beautiful village, set amongst hills and cotton fields. In a wide delta nearby are the fine, sloping sands of Iztuzu beach. Loggerhead turtles have nested here for hundreds of years and the beach is now a conservation area. The beach has now been discovered by tourists. They are rushing to this unspoilt corner of Turkey.

▲ **C** Adapted from a holiday brochure

◀ **D** Turtle beach at Dalyan

I'm a conservationist. My job is to protect wildlife. In the Mediterranean we help local people to understand the problems facing turtles. Sand was being taken from the beach to build new hotels. This has stopped now. Hotel lights upset turtles so screens were put up on the windows. Barriers stop people driving onto the beaches. Turtle watchers can only visit the beach at night in small groups, with a guide.

▲ **E** A conservationist with the World Wide Fund for Nature (WWF) explains how the turtles are protected

Can tourism and the environment work together?

In places like Zakynthos people need tourism for jobs and money. Tourists may stop coming if the environment is spoilt, so the landscape and wildlife must be protected.

WWF runs 25 major **conservation** projects in the Mediterranean. These projects help to look after wildlife and their environments. One example is a reserve in La Trapa, Majorca, where wild falcons, eagles and rare plants are protected. Other Mediterranean species are still in danger. The monk seal is killed by fisherman and the areas where it lives are being developed for tourism. There are fewer than 1000 monk seals left.

1 Name the Mediterranean countries where loggerhead turtles are found.

2 Use the information here and on pages 70–71 to list the ways in which tourists cause harm to the turtles.

3 Imagine you are on holiday in Dalyan.
   a) Make a postcard which shows a scene, or scenes, from Dalyan.
   b) Write home on the back of your card, describing your holiday. Mention a visit to the turtles.

4 Read E and F. Explain why local people are willing to work with the World Wide Fund for Nature (WWF).

▲ **F** The World Wide Fund for Nature (WWF) protects wildlife

The Mediterranean environment

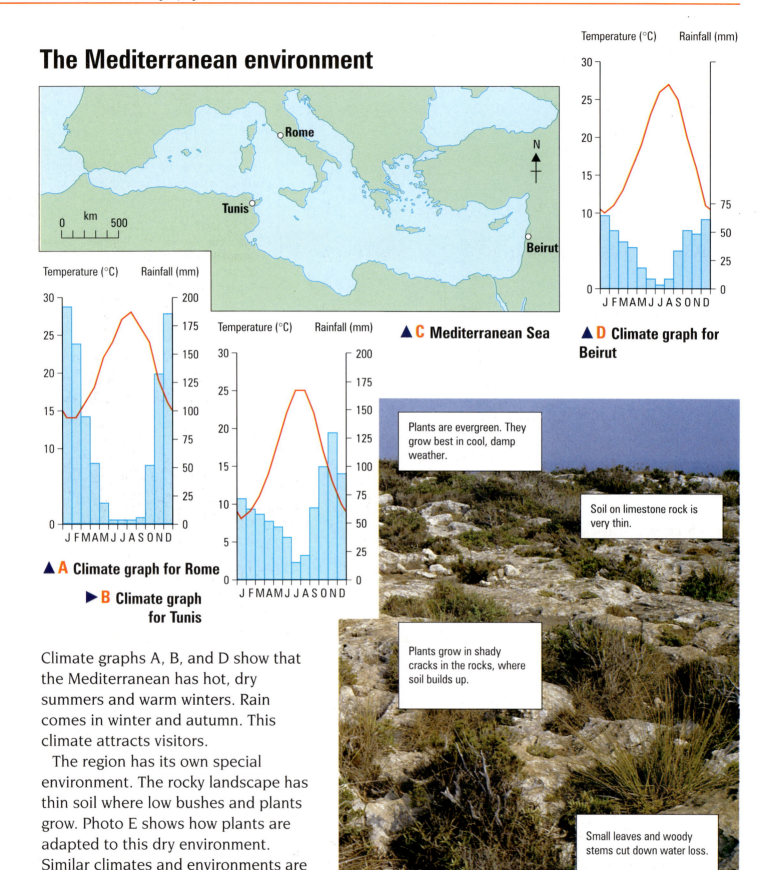

▲ **C** Mediterranean Sea

▲ **D** Climate graph for Beirut

▲ **A** Climate graph for Rome

▶ **B** Climate graph for Tunis

Climate graphs A, B, and D show that the Mediterranean has hot, dry summers and warm winters. Rain comes in winter and autumn. This climate attracts visitors.

The region has its own special environment. The rocky landscape has thin soil where low bushes and plants grow. Photo E shows how plants are adapted to this dry environment. Similar climates and environments are found in California, in the USA, and in Australia and South Africa.

Plants are evergreen. They grow best in cool, damp weather.

Soil on limestone rock is very thin.

Plants grow in shady cracks in the rocks, where soil builds up.

Small leaves and woody stems cut down water loss.

▲ **E** Mediterranean plants on Menorca, Spain

Why are there so few trees?

People have lived in the Mediterranean region for thousands of years. There were forests of cork, oak and pine but many have been cut down over the years. In places like Tunisia this deforestation is still happening.

In rural Tunisia wood fires are used to bake bread. Stoves waste wood, as they use only 10% of the wood's energy. They also fill homes with smoke. A study suggested these improvements.

- Bread could be baked on an improved stove, which villagers would share. 50% less wood would be used.
- Goats should be kept out of the forests because they damage young trees.
- New trees should be planted.

Using up the forests

In the mountains of north-west Tunisia, women spend about four hours each day collecting firewood. Every year each family burns 4.5 tonnes of wood just to bake bread. Trees have also been cut down by loggers and damaged by goats. More than 40% of the cork, oak and pine forests have been cut down in the last 40 years. This has caused soil erosion and underground water sources have dried up.

▲ **F** Extract adapted from *The Power to Change*, by Essma Ben Hamida, 1992

1 Describe three ways that plants are adapted to the hot, dry conditions in the Mediterranean.

2 Look at climate graphs A, B, and D. Which city:
a) is hottest in June
b) has the heaviest rainfall
c) has the coolest months?

3 Make a large copy of the table opposite. Give it the title 'Deforestation' and use Units 1, 3, and 5 to help fill it in.

	Kenya (page 53)	Ghana (pages 7, 15)	India (page 31)	Tunisia (page 75)
Reasons for deforestation				
Effects				
Action being taken				

▶ **G** Herding sheep and goats in Tunisia

Farming in the Mediterranean region

Hot dry summers can mean a shortage of water. Tourism, industry and farming all need water. Mediterranean farmers have always grown crops that do well in hot, dry weather, such as olives and grapes. Olive trees grow well in poor soils and have long roots that can find water deep underground.

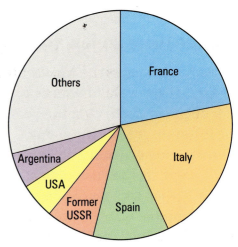

▲ **B** Wine producing countries

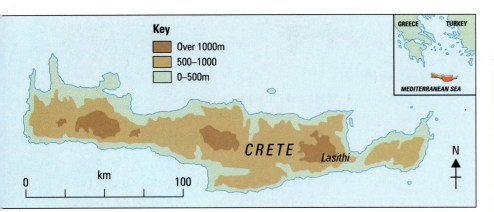

▲ **A** The island of Crete

Traditional farming in Crete

Crete is a Greek island in the eastern Mediterranean. It has dry, thin soils and rocky mountain slopes. Some parts of the island can only be reached by boat. It does not get regular rainfall, so lack of water can be a problem.

In the Lasithi Plain, windmills are used to pump water to the surface. The water is used to irrigate crops of olives, lemons, almonds and figs. Windmills are cheap and easy to run.

	Production	
Country	%	Tonnes (thousands)
Italy	31	3250
Spain	27	2891
Greece	17	1800
Turkey	8	800
Morocco	4	440
Tunisia	3	330

▲ **C** World olive production

▲ **D** The water windmills of Lasithi

1 Use B and C. Copy and complete the following sentences.
.... is the biggest producer of olives in the world with ...... %. It is also the *first/second/third* largest producer of wine. The Mediterranean region produces over ...... % of the world's wine.

2 Use the percentage figures in table C to draw a pie chart. Give your chart a title to explain what it shows.

The need for water in the Languedoc

The Languedoc region of France produces 40% of all French wine. But the poor soil gives poor grapes, so only cheap table wine is made. It sells for only four francs (50p) a litre.

Some farmers now earn more money by growing vegetables and soft fruit (such as peaches, apricots and strawberries). These crops need more water than grapes. More chemical fertilizers and pesticides are also used to grow them. Farmers need to be taught how to grow these crops. The European Union pays to train farmers.

Modern **irrigation** can be wasteful. Crops are irrigated using sprinklers and sprays. A lot of water is wasted. Chemicals are washed into rivers and pollute the sea.

▲ **F** Apricot trees in the Languedoc

3 Give one reason why farming in the Languedoc has changed.

4 Draw up a table to show the advantages and disadvantages of growing vines and olives in the Mediterranean.

5 List the environmental problems caused by growing new crops.

▶ **E** The Languedoc region of France

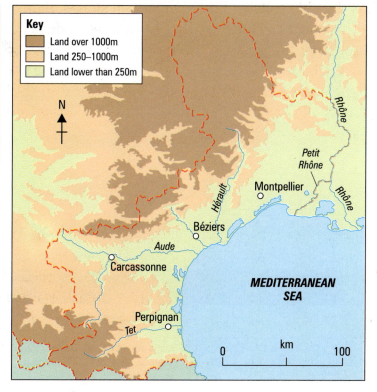

Key
Land over 1000m
Land 250–1000m
Land lower than 250m

FRANCE
ITALY
SPAIN
N

N

Rhône
Petit Rhône
Montpellier
Rhône
Hérault
Béziers
Aude
Carcassonne
MEDITERRANEAN SEA
Perpignan
Tet

0   km   100

A sinking city – Venice, Italy

The city of Venice in Italy faces huge difficulties. Over 50 million tourists come to Venice every year. They like the beautiful old buildings, art galleries and canals. But Venice was built on the soft mud of the River Po delta. Now it is slowly sinking into the polluted Mediterranean. The visitors bring wealth and jobs but they also add to the problems of waste and pollution. An enormous effort is needed by every country to save Venice from the problems caused by tourism, sewage and waste.

▼ **A** A false-colour satellite image of Venice

▲ **B** The canals and buildings of Venice

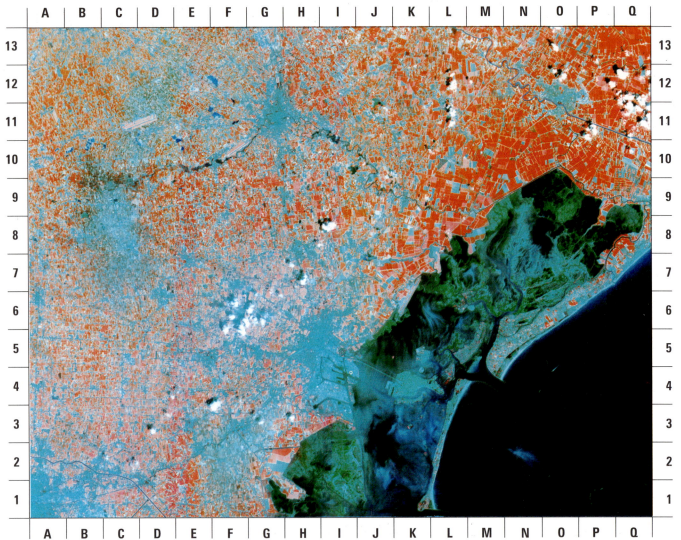

© CNES/SPOT Image

Fields show as red and pink. Nitrates from fertilizers run off into the sea.

Water shows as blue. Deeper water is almost black. Shallow water is a lighter blue.

Green areas in the sea show foul-smelling seaweed. This seaweed grows too well on the pollution from sewage and fertilizers.

The built-up areas of the city show as turquoise blue.

The future of the Mediterranean

Map C shows how serious the region's problems are. Many countries have got together to look for solutions. The European Union, the United Nations, and the World Bank met in 1990 and made a plan. It calls for:
- the control of industrial waste from Egypt
- controls for pollution and development in Turkey
- study and conservation of wildlife in the region.

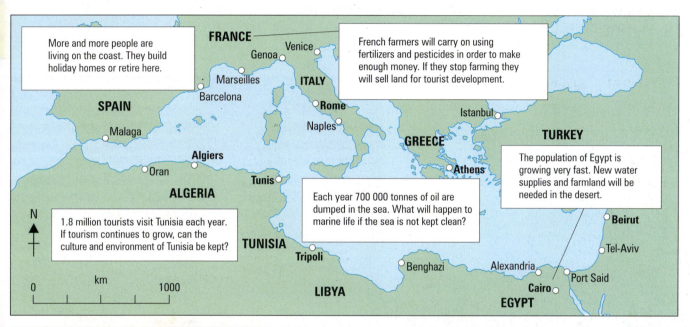

More and more people are living on the coast. They build holiday homes or retire here.

French farmers will carry on using fertilizers and pesticides in order to make enough money. If they stop farming they will sell land for tourist development.

1.8 million tourists visit Tunisia each year. If tourism continues to grow, can the culture and environment of Tunisia be kept?

Each year 700 000 tonnes of oil are dumped in the sea. What will happen to marine life if the sea is not kept clean?

The population of Egypt is growing very fast. New water supplies and farmland will be needed in the desert.

FRANCE · Venice · Genoa · Marseilles · Barcelona · ITALY · Rome · Naples · GREECE · Athens · Istanbul · TURKEY · SPAIN · Malaga · Algiers · Oran · Tunis · ALGERIA · TUNISIA · Tripoli · Benghazi · LIBYA · Alexandria · Cairo · Port Said · EGYPT · Beirut · Tel-Aviv

N

km
0   1000

▲ **C** Issues facing the Mediterranean area

1 What can be seen in photo B that would interest tourists?

2 Look at satellite photo A.

  a) Match the following features with the correct grid reference:

fields	I2
deep water	I5
shallow water	N10
seaweed	N4
buildings	K3

3 In what ways is Venice similar to Dalyan in Turkey? How is it different? Discuss:
  a) what brings the tourists
  b) the effects of tourism
  c) the threats to the environment.

Review

- The Mediterranean region is the most popular tourist area in the world.
- The region has its own climate and vegetation.
- Tourism, farming and industry need land and water. They also cause problems of waste and pollution.
- Many countries are joining together to save the Mediterranean but it is still in danger.

4 Study map C. Discuss the problems in the Mediterranean.

  a) Which problem do you think needs most urgent action? Give reasons for your choice.
  b) What makes it difficult to solve these problems?

8 Spain

Spain is a Mediterranean country. It faces many of the problems that we read about in Unit 7, such as the effects of tourism, and the demand for water.
- What is Spain like?
- How has Spain developed?
- How do regions vary?

► A Tourists on the Costa del Sol

▼ B Spain

Key
Height of the land (m)

N

	2000–4000
	1000–2000
	400–1000
	200–400
	0–200
	Sea level

0   100   200   300
km

UK

FRANCE

ATLANTIC OCEAN

Bay of Biscay

La Coruña

Cantabrian Mountains   Bilbao   Pyrenees

Ebro

Valladolid   Zaragoza   CATALONIA   Costa Brava

PORTUGAL   Madrid   Tajo   Barcelona

Lisbon   SPAIN   BALEARIC ISLANDS

Valencia

Sierra Morena

Guadalquivir   Murcia

Seville   Granada   Sierra Nevada   Costa Blanca

ANDALUSIA

Costa del Sol   MEDITERRANEAN

Gibraltar (UK)   ALGERIA

MOROCCO

What is Spain like?

Spain is changing very fast. In 1940 it was a poor, developing country where 52% of people worked in farming. Today, only 10% of the population work in farming. Tourism is now the most important industry. Spain's **economy** is the eighth biggest in the world. This means that its trade and industry are successful. But Spain also has the highest rate of unemployment in the European Union: 20% of its workers have no job.

Spain's landscape

Spain has long, sandy beaches, high plains and mountains. The Pyrenees in the north and the Sierra Nevada in the south are over 3000m high. Most of Spain is hot and dry.

Tourism

More tourists visit Spain than anywhere else in the world. Over 50 million tourists visit the country each year. This is even more than Spain's population of 39 million. Tourism employs 11% of Spanish people. Map C shows how important tourism is to each region of Spain.

▼ **C** The importance of tourism to Spain

Key
Hotel nights (millions), 1990

20+
10-20
3-10
2-3
1-2
Up to 1

Factfile: Spain	
Population:	39 200 000
Capital:	Madrid
Major imports:	Machinery, electrical equipment, fuels and chemicals
Major exports:	Cars and car parts, machinery, electrical equipment, vegetables and fruit

1 Use map B.
  a) Name the countries bordering Spain.
  b) Measure the distance from Madrid to Barcelona.

2 Copy the sentences, using maps B and C to fill in the gaps.
The most popular tourist resorts are the Costa .... in Andalusia, the .... in the south-east, and the northern .... in Catalonia. Popular islands are the .... off the coast of Valencia, and the .... islands.

▼ **D** Madrid, the capital city

Cheap holidays for everyone?

Millions of tourists come to Spain for its warm winters and hot summers. Package holidays were first introduced in the 1950s. Prices included flights, meals and a room. Choosing a holiday is very easy nowadays. Travel agents offer cheap flights and package holidays. Many people can now afford holidays in Spain.

1 Compare photos A and B.
a) List the differences you can see.
b) Which do you prefer, Benidorm in photo A or photo B?

2 Look at graph C. In which month would you like to visit Almeria? Why?

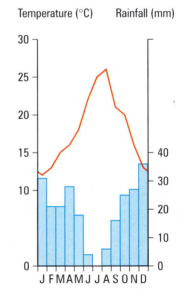

◄ **C** Climate graph for the tourist resort of Almeria, Costa del Sol

▲ **A** Benidorm was a fishing village before it was developed into a tourist resort

► **B** The resort of Benidorm today

Different holidays

Not all tourists want hot, crowded beaches. Some people visit Spain's historic cities such as Madrid or Seville. Others visit the cooler Atlantic coast shown in photo E. Many people visit Spain in winter, when it is warmer than their own country. You can read about this in article D.

▼ **D** There are holidays in Spain to suit most people

▲ **E** The coast of Galicia, northern Spain

Escaping the British winter

Many retired people like to spend the winter abroad. A holiday in Spain means they can avoid the cold wet months in England, and have fun at the same time. Many travel agents offer long stay holidays at cheap rates during the winter months. Hotels run special activities such as cookery lessons, bingo, darts and keep-fit classes for their older guests. The Costa Blanca and the Costa del Sol are both popular for this type of winter holiday.

Where people are from	Number of nights (in millions) stayed in hotels			
	Balearics	Madrid	Malaga	Tenerife
Spain	9.2	3.8	6.4	3.6
UK	8.8	–	1.4	3.0
Germany	12.2	–	0.6	1.4
France	3.2	–	1.0	0.8
Others	6.4	3.0	2.8	2.1

▲ **F** Different resorts attract people from different countries

3 Use photos B and E. Describe the ways in which Benidorm is different, or similar to Galicia. You may use the words below to help.

peaceful   crowded   calm   busy
quiet   busy   unspoilt

4 a) Discuss the kinds of holidays the following people might like in Spain.

(i) a family with young children
(ii) a group of young single people
(iii) an older couple without children.
Think of the sorts of activities they would want, and the facilities they would need.

b) Which resort might these people like best, E or B? Give reasons for your answer.

Different regions

Spain is made up of seventeen regions. Each region has its own climate, culture, and language. Some parts of Spain have grown wealthy, but others are among the poorest areas in the European Union. To show how uneven Spain's development has been, the country can be split into four regions. Map A shows these four regions.

◄ A The economy of Spain

1 Growing Spain
- Many new jobs in service industries
- Modern farming
- Modern industry

2 Spain in crisis
- Old industries are failing
- Steel plants and coal mines have closed
- Rising unemployment

3 Unchanging Spain
- No new industry
- Farms still grow traditional crops such as olives
- Underdeveloped

4 Shrinking Spain
- Many people are moving away
- High percentage of elderly people
- Little work
- Farming is hard in mountainous areas

Key
- ■ Growing Spain
- ■ Spain in crisis
- ■ Unchanging Spain
- ■ Shrinking Spain

Key
GNP per person US $
- ■ 14 000–15 999
- ■ 12 000–13 999
- ■ 10 000–11 999
- ■ 8 000–9 999

◄ B Wealth in Spain

1 Use map B. What is the average income in:
   a) Andalusia
   b) Catalonia
   c) the Balearic Islands?
2 Which parts of Spain are growing?

▲ **D** Industrial Spain

▲ **E** Andalusia, Spain

Andalusia – Spain's poorest region

Andalusia is the poorest, least developed area of Spain. Tourism employs 60% of workers. Farming is the next most important money-earner. But unemployment is still high and average incomes are low.

Andalusia has long sandy beaches, high mountains and desert. Farming is important and new methods and new crops have been introduced. For example, flowers, fruit and vegetables are grown in plastic greenhouses. In Almeria 250 million kilos of crops are produced this way. Most crops are exported to other European countries.

The Guadalquivir

The River Guadalquivir has its source in the mountains of Andalusia. From its source it flows west 700km to the Atlantic Ocean. There it forms a delta 160km wide. There is little rain in Andalusia so water is taken 1025km from the River Tajo, near Madrid, to Audalusia. Tourism and farming both demand water.

3 Why does water have to be brought to Andalusia from other parts of Spain?

▲ **C** Strawberries growing in plastic greenhouses, Almeria

Coto de Doñana

Agriculture and tourism sometimes fight to use the same resources. Both of these industries need water but it is in short supply in the area. Also, the environment can suffer when these industries develop.

▲ **B**
The imperial eagle may die out

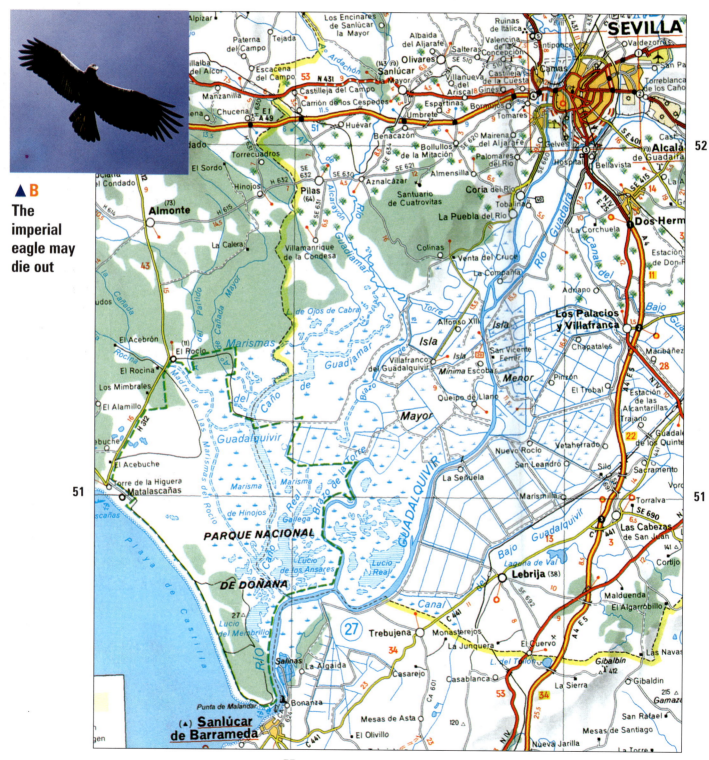

1 Use map A.
  a) What town is at the mouth of the Guadalquivir?
  b) On which side of the river is the National Park, west or east?

2 a) Use article C to list three environments found in the National Park.
  b) Give a grid reference on map A where you might find:
    a) sand dunes
    b) marsh land.

Coto de Doñana sanctuary is drying up

Coto de Doñana is a famous **wetland** wildlife sanctuary. The National Park contains marsh, coastal woodland and sand dunes. The endangered Spanish lynx and the rare imperial eagle are found here, as are thousands of water birds.

Today the Coto de Doñana is in danger of drying up. It is threatened by rice farming, pollution from insecticides, fertilizers and tourism.

▲ **C** Extract adapted from the *World Wide Fund for Nature newsletter*

Farming, tourism, or conservation?

Farmers in Andalusia irrigate their crops. Irrigation is very wasteful: a lot of water evaporates or soaks through the sandy soil. As more crops are grown, more water is needed. Using too much of the water beneath the ground (ground water) could lower the **water table**. Diagram D shows the serious environmental problems this might cause.

Tourism would bring much needed work and money. A new tourist resort is planned at Matalascanas. But more tourists mean even more water will be used. The average tourist uses 300 litres of water per day. The Doñana National Park needs that water to survive.

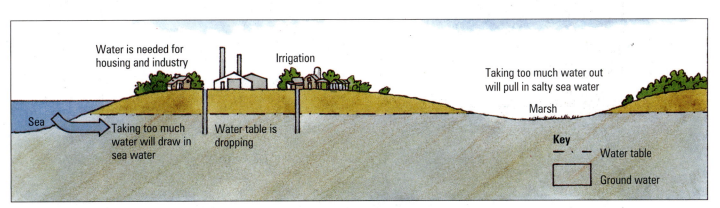

▲ **D** How using too much ground water changes the environment

3 Imagine you are one of the following people:
  a) a farmer
  b) a hotel owner
  c) a conservationist.

Write about how you might feel about more tourist development near the Doñana National Park.

Catalonia – Spain's richest region

Catalonia is the richest part of Spain. It has the most industry, and produces 20% of Spain's wealth. Most of Catalonia's population live along the coast, or in the city of Barcelona. In the north, the mountains of the Pyrenees form a border with France. In the dry south, the River Ebro creates a delta as it meets the Mediterranean, as map C shows.

Using up the water

Like Andalusia, Catalonia has a water resource problem. Rainfall is heaviest in the north and west, but most people live on the drier coast. Water is taken out of the rivers Ebro and Llobregat. It is used for cities, farming and industry. Demand for water rises as farmers irrigate more and more land. New tourist developments also demand water.

▲ **B** Catalonia

1 Use map C.
  a) In which direction does the River Ebro flow:
    (i) in Tortosa?
    (ii) where it reaches the sea?
  b) What is made by the River Ebro as it reaches the sea?

▼ **A** The Pyrenees in Spain

▼ **C** The River Ebro and its delta

Barcelona

Welcome to Barcelona! Our city is on the beautiful Mediterranean coast. It has a mild, pleasant climate. Barcelona is famous for its wonderful buildings, fine art museums and large parks. We call it the second city of Spain and the centre of Catalonia.

▲ **D**

In the 1960s and 1970s Barcelona grew rapidly as people moved in from rural areas. Most people came from rural parts of Catalonia. Many more came from poor regions of Andalusia. Many had to live in shanty towns and took poorly paid jobs on building sites. The poor shanty towns have now been replaced by blocks of flats.

▲ **F** Square in central Barcelona

Factfile: Barcelona

- The city has a population of over 4 million people, with 2 million living in the centre.
- Cloth, publishing, fashion, and car production are its major industries.
- The 1992 Olympics were held in the city.
- Barcelona has a very famous football team!

▶ **G**

The growth of Barcelona's population

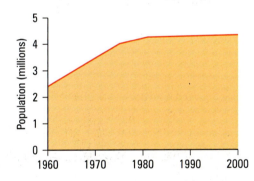

▼ **E** Shanty housing in the early 1980s

2 What activities can tourists enjoy in Barcelona? Use D and F to help you.

3 What was Barcelona's population in:
a) 1960   **b)** 1980?

4 How much did the population grow between 1960 and 1980? Give reasons for this growth.

5 Look at photo E. Describe the difficulties a family living in shanty housing might face.

Developing industry in Catalonia

Most new industry has been built along the Mediterranean coast. The strip from Catalonia to Valencia and down to Murcia produces 44% of Spain's exports.

Barcelona

Barcelona is the main industrial city in Catalonia. It is attractive to foreign companies because:

- they are offered good sites between the port and airport
- these sites are free of certain taxes
- wages are low.

Tourists like Barcelona because:

- the 1992 Olympic games were held there
- it has beach resorts nearby
- it has theatres, museums and historic buildings.

▼ **A** **A new car factory built close to a railway line behind the city**

Development has brought jobs and money to the city. It has also caused problems for the environment. Car exhaust fumes pollute the air and raw sewage pollutes the sea.

Barcelona continues to develop, but faces these problems:

- control of pollution
- demand for more and more water
- lack of space because of the mountains to the north and west.

Photo A shows a new development, a car factory built above the city.

Spain in the wider world

Spain joined the European Economic Community in 1986. Foreign companies like General Motors came to Spain, attracted by its low wages. This **foreign investment** means that money is put into Spanish companies by foreign firms. As a result, Spain has the eighth biggest economy in the world.

Changes in wealth

The average income, or amount of money a person earns per week, has doubled in Spain since 1984, and is still rising. Spain expects that its average income will equal that of the UK by the year 2000.

◀ **B** **Growth in Spanish exports**

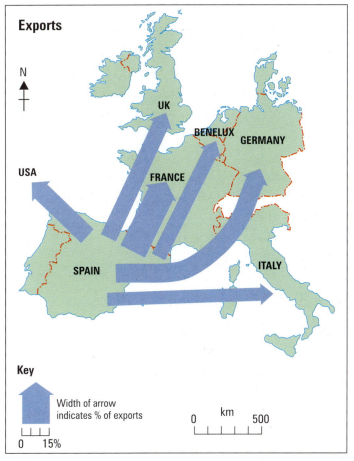

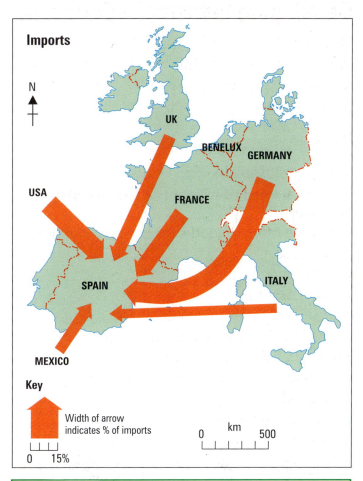

▲ **C** Spain's exports and imports

1 Use map C.
  a) Where do most of Spain's exports go?
  b) How much goes to the UK?
  c) Where do most of Spain's imports come from?

Review

- Each region of Spain has its different landscapes, work and wealth.
- Spain is changing. Fewer people are employed in farming, yet more land is being irrigated. Demand for water is rising.
- Tourism is Spain's most important service industry and has created many jobs. The demand for water and the growth of the tourist industry are affecting the environment.

2 Write a report on Spain including pictures, diagrams and maps. Use these headings: Changes in Spain, Tourism Work, Farming.

9 The European Union

EUROPE

Fifteen countries make up the European Union (EU).
Map A shows the countries that:
- were EU members in 1994
- joined in 1995
- wish to join in the future.

▶ **A**
European Union membership

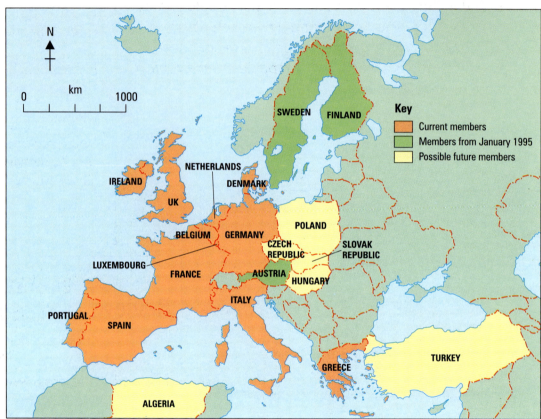

N

km
0   1000

SWEDEN   FINLAND

Key
- Current members
- Members from January 1995
- Possible future members

IRELAND
NETHERLANDS
DENMARK

UK

BELGIUM   GERMANY
POLAND

LUXEMBOURG
CZECH REPUBLIC   SLOVAK REPUBLIC

FRANCE   AUSTRIA
HUNGARY

ITALY

PORTUGAL
SPAIN

GREECE
TURKEY

ALGERIA

What does the EU do?

European Union countries work together.
- They agree how much each type of farm should produce in each EU country. This makes sure that people have enough milk, wheat and vegetables. It also makes sure that farmers are paid fair prices.
- They make travel and trade easy between EU countries. This helps businesses to sell their goods.
- They help areas of high unemployment in the EU. Money is given to help development in these areas.

1 Use map A to list:
a) EU member countries
b) countries who may join.

Helping poorer areas

Some EU countries are richer than others. As table C shows, Germany is much richer than Portugal. Some areas such as Spain, have both rich and poor areas. The EU gives money to poorer areas. These areas are either:
- industrial areas where jobs have been lost when old industries closed down
- rural areas where there are few jobs and facilities.

Merseyside in the UK receives help from the EU. It will be given £1600 million over the next five years. People can be trained in new skills and new technology to help them to find work. Transport to the area will be improved. These developments should attract new companies to the area and create more jobs.

Current members	GNP (US $) per person	People per doctor
Germany	23 650	370
Greece	6 230	580
Ireland	10 780	630
Italy	18 580	210
Portugal	5 620	490
UK	16 750	300
Countries which have applied to join		
Turkey	1 820	1 260
Poland	1 830	490
Hungary	2 690	340

▲ **C** Variations in wealth between some EU countries

▼ **B** Regions of the EU that receive help

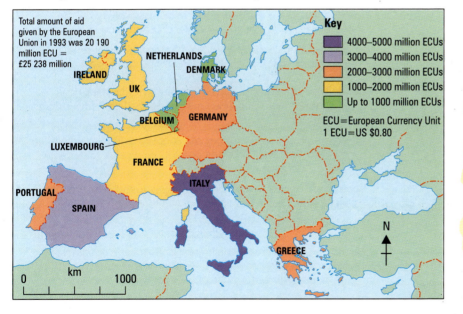

Merseyside grasps EU lifeline

Merseyside has a terrible unemployment problem. It has been caused by the loss of unskilled jobs on the docks, and the closing down of big manufacturing companies. In Bootle, almost half the adult male population is jobless.

▲ **D** From *The Times*, 2 November 1994

2 In which ways does the EU help poorer areas?

3 a) Using table B, draw a bar chart to show the wealth of Germany, Portugal, Greece, and Poland.

b) Copy the sentences opposite, using your chart to help choose the right words.

Germany has much *more/less* wealth than Portugal and Greece. Poland is much *richer/poorer* than many current EU members.

4 The EU wishes to help poorer *regions* but may not want poorer *countries* like Turkey to join. Discuss possible reasons for this.

Glossary

Accessible Easy to reach, either by road or rail.

Agroforestry Mixing farming and forestry without destroying the rainforest.

Air quality How clean, or safe the air is. Poor air quality means high levels of pollution.

Birth rate The number of babies born each year for every 1000 people.

Canopy The thick layer of leaves at the top of a forest. It cuts out most of the sunlight and protects the forest floor from heavy rain.

Climate The average weather conditions of a place or region over many years. It is worked out from daily weather records.

Colonize When plants start to grow on a new area of land.

Conservation The study and protection of wildlife and the environment.

Coral reef Corals are tiny sea animals with a hard outer skeleton. Large colonies of different types of coral form reefs in warm, shallow seas.

Cyclones Violent storms which start over the sea in tropical regions. High winds, heavy rain, and large waves cause flooding and destruction in coastal areas.

Deposition The sea deposits mud, and sand on the shore as a beach. Rivers also deposit sediment.

Deforestation The cutting down of trees and the clearing of forest areas. The timber may be sold or used for firewood, or the land may be used for farming or mining.

Developed countries Countries with wealthy economies and a high percentage of people living in urban areas.

Developing countries Countries with poorer economies where many people live in rural areas.

Economy The economy of a country is its trade, industry, and money.

Ecosystem A community of plants and animals, and the environment in which they live. Each part of the ecosystem depends on the others.

Environment The surroundings in which people, animals, and plants live. It may be a natural environment like a rainforest or savanna, or it may be an urban environment like a city.

Equator An imaginary line around the middle of the Earth which represents the 0° line of latitude.

Erosion The wearing away of the Earth's surface by the action of rivers, ice, sea, or wind.

Estuary The mouth of a river where fresh water meets salty sea water.

Exports Goods which are made in one country and sold to other countries.

Fertilizers Manure or chemicals put onto the land to improve the soil so that plants will grow well.

Foreign investment When foreign companies spend their money abroad setting up new branches and building factories.

Gross National Product (GNP) A measurement of a country's wealth.

Habitat The natural environment of a plant or animal.

Hawkers People who sells goods on the streets, often moving from place to place.

Hurricane Violent tropical storm.

Hydro-electric power (HEP) Electricity produced by the force of fast-moving water. This water drives turbines which make electricity.

Informal work Work which does not have a regular wage, or where the worker does not pay taxes, e.g. selling on the streets without a licence, or collecting and recycling rubbish.

Irrigation Transporting water to an area where there is a shortage of water, so that growing crops can have water.

Landslide The sudden movement of earth and rock down a hill or mountain. Landslides may be started by heavy rain or deforestation.

Life expectancy The number of years the average person can expect to live. This depends on diet, medical facilities, housing, and type of work.

Location The place where something is found. The location of Ghana is in West Africa.

Logging Cutting down trees to sell as wood or timber.

Mangrove trees Trees which grow on tropical coastlines, where rivers enter the sea. They are the only trees which can grow where sea water mixes with river water.

Manufacturing industry Making goods such as stereos, computers, televisions, cars, or parts of goods, e.g. computer chips.

Migration When people move away from their homes, usually in search of work. Animals and birds also migrate.

Mudslides Heavy rain or melting snow turn soil and rocks into flowing liquid mud.

Organic farming No artificial fertilizers or pesticides are used.

Plantations A large area of land used to grow one type of crop such as tea, sugar, coffee, or trees for timber.

Pollution When water, land, or air is made dirty by waste, e.g. rubbish, sewage, industrial waste, and exhaust fumes.

Population density The number of people per area of land (usually per km^2).

Raw materials The natural materials needed to make things, e.g. timber, oil, or iron ore.

Renewable resource Types of resource which will not run out.

Rural areas Country areas where most people live in villages and small towns.

Savanna A grassy plain with few or no trees found in tropical and subtropical regions.

Sediment Pieces of rock which are carried and then dropped by water, wind, or ice.

Settlement A group of houses and other buildings. It may be just a few homes or a large city.

Service Helping or serving someone, e.g. in a shop or restaurant. Service companies sell their services rather than make products, e.g. transport and banking.

Shanty towns Another name for squatter settlements.

Smog A fog caused when damp air mixes with air pollution such as smoke or car fumes.

Squatter settlement A settlement which has been built by people who live on land that does not belong to them.

Storm surges Waves that flood coastal areas, caused by a rise in the level of the sea due to strong winds.

Tide The regular change in the level of the sea on the shore. The time when the level of the sea is highest is known as high tide, the lowest is low tide.

Tropical rainforests Forests that grow near the Equator, where there is high rainfall and temperatures above 25°C. At least half of the world's species of wildlife live in the rainforests.

Typhoon A violent storm which starts over the sea in tropical regions. High winds, heavy rain, and large waves cause flooding in coastal areas.

Unemployment When people are unable to find work.

Urban areas Built-up areas, towns or cities.

Urban heat island Towns and cities are slightly warmer in the centre than in the surrounding countryside because of heat given out by roads and buildings.

Water table The level of water in the ground. It can be lower or higher depending on how much rain has fallen and how much water has been used.

Weather The conditions such as the temperature, amount of rain, or sunshine.

Weathering The breaking down of rocks caused by the effects of the weather and atmosphere.

Wetland A marshy or boggy piece of land that may be flooded with water in the rainy season.

Index